Every Hunter Wants To Know

Every Hunter Wants To Know

A *Leningrad Life*

MIKHAIL IOSSEL

W·W·NORTON & COMPANY · *New York London*

Some of the stories in this collection have appeared elsewhere, in slightly different form: "Beyond the Pale" in *The Agni Review*; "Counterbalance" in *The North American Review*; "Every Hunter Wants To Know" in *Tikkun*; "Dog Days" in *The Threepenny Review*; "Bologoye" in *Boulevard*.

The author would like to express his gratitude for their friendship and support to the following people: Sergei Artiouchkov, Peter Cole, Sara Dickinson, August Kleinzahler, Fred Leebron, and Jonah Winter.

Printed in the United States of America.

The text of this book is composed in Aster,
with the display set in Benguiat Medium.
Composition and manufacturing by
The Maple-Vail Book Manufacturing Group.
Book design by Jacques Chazaud.

First Edition.

Library of Congress Cataloging-in-Publication Data

Iossel, Mikhail.
Every hunter wants to know : a Leningrad life / Mikhail Iossel.
p. cm.
1. Leningrad (R.S.F.S.R.)—History—1917– —Fiction. I. Title.
PS3559.O8E9   1991
813'.54—dc20   90–28352

ISBN 0–393–02985–9

W.W. Norton & Company, Inc.
500 Fifth Avenue, New York, N.Y. 10110
W.W. Norton & Company, Ltd.
10 Coptic Street, London WC1A 1PU

1 2 3 4 5 6 7 8 9 0

To the memory of
Thomas Williams

Contents

Beyond the Pale

Where can you come from in the Pale
that's so different from where you're going?

MALAMUD, *The Fixer*

The first American I met in my life was a man named Bruce, an exchange student of Russian from New York, who had drifted into my friend's spacious old Leningrad communal apartment one white night in June 1979, smiling absent-mindedly, drawn by the sounds of Western rock music and loud party laughter from the window, well past his dormitory curfew and in keeping with the popular belief that anything can happen on a White Night.

Indeed, anything can happen on a white night in Leningrad: the purple sails cover the river, the bridges are thrown open, a militiaman smiles shyly, checking passports—but a foreigner in the room? We were stunned. A brief pause of uninterrupted music followed. Then the most sober of the guests began to dance around the American. I knew some English and introduced myself to him. We exchanged a handshake. He shouted his name and age into my ear: twenty-four. "What a coincidence!" I shouted back. "I'm twenty-four, too!" We retreated to the open window, smiling at each other.

I had no experience talking to non-Soviets. My English was inadequate, and his Russian was poor, but it didn't really matter, because the very fact—and act—of standing next to a foreigner was of supreme importance to me. This is not to say that I had never seen foreigners before: I had, but, of course, I never approached one. I wasn't crazy. Foreigners were bad news and spelled trouble, and I wasn't looking for trouble that summer, even though I couldn't say—exactly what I was looking for.

Living in Leningrad, "Venice of the North," the most un-Russian of all Soviet cities, one can't help noticing the chirping flocks of foreign tourists, with their expensive cameras, everywhere on Nevsky Prospect (the city's Main Street), usually followed by the compact and conspiratorial flocks of adolescent black marketeers. But I was not a black marketeer. I had a well-developed sense of normal fear. Starting the conversation with Bruce, I knew full well that he might spell a lot of trouble for me, since I had been officially proscribed from contact with foreigners by the research institute that I had been sent to work for upon graduation from college. Like most research institutes, they had each new employee sign a printed promise to alert their KGB representative in Department One immediately after accidental contact with a foreigner took place. It made almost no difference to Department One, concerned as they were with the enforcement of their policy, whether the foreigner was a Bulgarian or an American, a brother-internationalist or a capitalist, tolerated because he was stuffed with hard currency.

An intentional contact with a foreigner was not even mentioned in the pledge: it was utterly unimaginable. But even an innocuous contact, once hastily reported to the KGB, would get an obedient fool into trouble. The KGB, in order to keep up the standards of common awareness, never took those episodes lightly and would immediately strike a hapless individual out of the mainstream, where life was relatively cozy and easy and one's job was secure. A comfortable apartment, even a boxy room in a communal apartment, was too priceless a possession to lose. There was a significant amount of fear in the air back in 1979.

No wonder that while socializing with Bruce over the vodka in our teacups, I was tense. My choices were obvious: either to stay and keep talking, hoping that it would never become known where it shouldn't, or the wiser choice, to bow out with a cold apology. I knew (or at least suspected) that the KGB was omnipotent, omnipresent, omniscient. Like most of the people who had never dealt with them (my parents, for instance, who would listen to the "Voice of America" in Russian in the dark of night), I held the KGB's all-pervasiveness in extremely high esteem. I knew (or at least suspected) that they could easily be watching Bruce and me through their infrared telescopes from across the river. But I was drinking vodka, and vodka has never failed to make me braver and more reckless than I actually am, or should have been, and I was talking to a real foreigner, born on the other side of the globe, in what is called the "Abroad" in Soviet vernacular, raised among unknown words and tales, and ideas, and whatnot ... a Martian of sorts: I was curious and excited, full of anticipation. Besides, I had always wanted to be a free man, free to talk to any foreigner, free to stop growing tense and hesitant whenever a foreigner happened into the field of my vision. I needed a chance, an opportunity, a push in the back—and I seemed to know what would happen next: I would find out, with anger and resentment, that there's no real difference between us, him and me, and then nothing would ever dupe me back into the misery of xenophobia again. Making up for a lifetime of near-ignorance, I was willing to take a risk. And so I stayed.

Besides the fact that it existed, all I knew about the

Abroad were the books from my parents' library that I had read—hundreds, or maybe thousands of them . . . hundreds, of course, not thousands—and naturally, the name of The Abroad's ultimate destructor, that pale stalking specter of communism from Karl Marx's "Manifesto," hammered hard into our gullible heads at school. (As I recall, at school, in our private conversations, we used to crack jokes about the imminent destruction of capitalism: "You know, capitalism is rotting and decaying, but its smell is so wonderful!") We had turned into cynical brats long before becoming members of the Komsomol, or Young Communist League: the pressure had been too strong not to provoke a backlash. However, one shouldn't underestimate the power of indoctrination—or rather, of a lopsided education; I can attest to that: in 1986, at thirty, stepping out of the plane in Frankfurt, two hours after I left the Soviet Union, I wandered idly around the Frankfurt airport. Against my prior belief, the dirt on the concrete floor was no cleaner in the West than in Leningrad. As I looked at the unbridled bright crowds of the Westerners in their habitat with indistinct irritation, I was surprised by a long-forgotten thought: "They just don't know that according to Marx their world has no future, that they're historically doomed, all of them!"

Talking to Bruce in the wee hours of the white morning in 1979, I knew all along about his being historically doomed, and I was jealous. I felt guilty. I rooted for a historic underdog, destined to be squashed by the ruthless wheels of the most advanced social theory. I wished vaguely I were historically doomed myself, too. But I was not, and neither was anyone I knew. The Abroad had nothing to do with us. The only person I knew who had been abroad was my mother: she had gone on a tourist trip to Czechoslovakia in 1968, a couple of months before our August tanks destroyed the Prague Spring. For me, a thirteen year old, it was a reasonably nice August, even in the shadow of the

thick black headlines splashed on the pages of the *Pravda*
my grandfather held in his hands on the terrace of a rented
summer house in Roshchino, near Leningrad. He nodded
his head contentedly: "Way to go! We should've done it
earlier!" He was an old bolshevik.

There are not many old bolsheviks around anymore.
My grandfather was seventy when he died. He joined the
Party at the age of seventeen or eighteen, right after the
revolution of 1917—the GOSR, the Great October Socialist
Revolution of our school textbooks. My grandfather was a
revolutionary, a man of rigid beliefs. He was a commissar
during World War II. His adoration of Stalin remained
unshaken at a time when most of his Party friends were
being shot down in Lubyanka's corridors with Stalin's name
on their bloodied lips. When Stalin was denounced by
Khrushchev in his secret speech, my grandfather probably
was badly hurt. This was a bad time for people like him.

My mother once told me an interesting, revealing story
about her parents and Stalin. The way I remember it is
that when the news of Stalin's death was broken on the
radio, that ubiquitous black dish on a white wall in the
kitchen, in March 1953 (Stalin had been dead for at least a
week by that time), my grandfather burst into uncontrol-
lable tears. The whole country was weeping. Sobbing, he
walked from the kitchen into his and my grandmother's
room in their Moscow communal apartment, where my
grandmother, upon hearing the same news on the radio,
was rejoicing. "Thank God! At last! That butcher!" she
exclaimed. She was a shrewd, but also a very cautious
woman normally, the wife of a Party functionary. My
grandfather had always thought, of course, that she, too,
loved Stalin, like everybody else: not loved, not even adored,
but rather cherished, worshiped him. As it turned out, he
discovered she never did, and now, under the influence of
an overwhelming moment, she got carried away. She must

have thought that my grandfather was still in the kitchen. But he was standing teary-eyed behind her back in their room, ready to share her grief. Her exclamation hit him hard. He was flabbergasted. "I can't believe my ears! I've lived with an enemy of the people all these years!" he erupted. (I should mention here that "ears" and "years" don't rhyme in Russian and his words didn't sound funny to either of them.) My grandmother turned around, bit her tongue, and cursed her stupidity. But it was too late; he had already left, dramatically slamming the door shut behind him—gone forever. . . .

For a year, I was told.

He went away for a year.

A year doesn't sound right to me—too epic. A day— maybe; or even possibly a week. Hot-tempered people are rarely persistent in their wrath—and my grandfather was hot-tempered, but never in a bad or unpredictable way. On the contrary, he was one of the nicest, kindest men I've ever known, although I've never known him as a fearsome zealot, ready to die and to kill for the revolution, and he never knew me as a budding enemy of the people—because that's what the emigrants are to the old bolsheviks: enemies of the people. Thank God, I never applied for an exit visa while he was alive. I didn't in any serious way contribute to his confusion during the 1970s, when everything went so wrong with the world that he had helped to build. His name was Rafail Zalmanovich Schub. He had changed it for a more Russian Fyodor Zakharovich shortly after the Great October of 1917, because the revolution of the classes was not supposed to distinguish its soldiers by their race. He died in 1975. I think he had traveled abroad, by the way.

My grandfather: of course! He had been abroad—in Berlin, strolling idly down Unter-den-Linden, hand in hand with my grandmother, his wife. Which means that she, too, was abroad once. Of course. They were there; my grandfather was then a victorious colonel of the Soviet Army at the close of World War II. My mother used to keep several trophy albums, full of schmaltzy, incredibly cozy German prewar postcards, on the bottom of the bookshelves in our apartment. She still keeps them, I'm sure. People get old and die, but those little pink kitschy turn-of-the-century Gretchens with their cloudlike lambs are going to outlive everyone.

So it's not as if our family had no relationships whatsoever with the Abroad. I was not the first one of us to cross the border with another country. And yet, the Abroad my mother and her parents saw wasn't a real Abroad. The part of Berlin where my grandfather had walked later became the capital of the GDR, East Germany; my mother's Czechoslovakia, needless to say, was—and is, at least at the time of this writing—the Socialist Republic. But what about the rest of the world? I suspected that none of us had ever been there. After all, ours was not a family of globetrotters. We were regular Soviets. We never seriously questioned life, because it was not likely to provide us with any answers. We believed that there was nothing wrong with spending one's whole life in one place and never being able to leave it. There was no point in having a dream that couldn't be realized. The Abroad, largely nonexisting as far as our family was concerned, was for other people, like Bruce. We'd seen those other people many times on TV.

We started getting together, Bruce and I, and some of his American exchange-student friends, that summer. We would talk, and drink, and talk, and get drunk—never in public places, though: usually in my apartment. I was lucky to have an apartment of my own. It was on the fifth floor of a solid gray apartment house built in the 1940s by German POWs. Talking and drinking with Americans, I tried to be very cautious—and not to give a damn at the same time. This wasn't easy. But something had turned in my perplexed mind: it was sad to know that all I could ever be was a nontraveling, scared Soviet.

Bruce was Jewish. I told him about my grandparents. They were born within the Pale of Settlement—Ukraine and Byelorussia, where the majority of Russian Jews used to live before the revolution, working hard in order to make ends meet. "What a coincidence!" he exclaimed. "My grandparents are from the Pale, too!" Soon we made another discovery, which seemed to both of us meaningful, amazing, and amusing: his grandparents, as it turned out, were born and raised in the same Byelorussian towns of the Pale where my grandparents were born and raised—Gomel and Bobruisk. Some coincidence, indeed!

It may sound a bit forced, as is often the case with certain types of uninvented circumstances, but I should also mention here that Bruce and I looked pretty much like each other—or rather, like two young men with a common lineage in their family charts, which, of course, we didn't have. Then again, all people are relatives, aren't they?

Bruce found it highly symbolic, but to me, being an American's almost-look-alike was only interesting in an abstract, educationally revealing way: it proved that people from quite different linguistic (shouldn't a foreign native language somehow rearrange one's mouth and jawline?) and political systems could actually pass for each other; no language, no ideology or lifelong history of steadfast undernourishment could prevent people from at least resembling, if not being, each other. "Genetics beats geography!" I'd thought enthusiastically. Today, I'm not so sure. The truth is, Sovietness marks one for life. There's always something about us fellow ex-compatriots that makes us instantly recognizable to each other. It's that timid and hopelessly defiant stare we give each other when our eyes meet, or, more often, don't meet in a foreign crowd—we recognize each other without looking each other in the eyes.

And it's also the way we walk, woodenly and naturally constrained, as if millions of disapproving eyes like ours are watching us.

We kept talking. Bruce was clearly much more impressed by the accidental coincidence of our origins than I could ever be—in part, I guess, because a foreigner's world is generally more possible, more open to life's bizarre opportunities, than a Soviet's. My imagination had never strayed far enough from Leningrad to get me interested in the idea of having been born in the Abroad. It simply couldn't happen, and there was no point in getting carried away.

"Imagine, you could have been born there, and I could have been born here!" Bruce would exclaim, confusing his "here" with my "there." "How come you're here? How come I'm there? That's wild!" He rolled his eyes.

I couldn't understand his excitement. I was where I was because I was born here, and I had to stay where I was, at least for a while. If I had applied for a "Jewish" exit visa, my father's career as a scientist would be in jeopardy, and my own career as a scientist-to-be would be over. I still had things to lose. I needed time to prepare my parents and to occupy the lowest rung on the social ladder and turn into an outcast, with absolutely nothing to fear. "I would love to emigrate, Bruce," I said. He only smiled. He was about to leave for America. It was his home simply because his grandparents had been taken there by their parents during the years of massive emigration from Ukraine and Byelorussia in the early twentieth century. My grandparents were not so fortunate.

Or unfortunate. Who knows? You can't replay your ancestors' lives after they are over. The only life you can— and maybe should—experiment with, is your own. I told Bruce an unverifiable story from our family's past, in which my grandmother's parents had, indeed, decided to emigrate to America during the Great Rush from the Pale. It was in 1909, or 1910. They had sold their house and all their salable belongings in order to pay their way from Odessa, the nearest seaport, to New York City, but rains, heavy and unexpected, had turned the day-long horsecart road into an impassable mess. My ancestors never made it to Odessa in time, and the ship left Russian shores without them.

Bruce shook his head in disbelief. "That's wild! They must've been totally crushed!" he said.

"Not totally, Bruce," I said reasonably, the way people talk to foreigners, when and if they do. "I really don't think so. Because they had survived. After all, what choice did they have but to keep living? They didn't commit suicide. My grandmother met and married my grandfather, and my mother was born. Twenty-two years later my mother met and married my father in Leningrad, and I was born. We're one happy family, and unless I emigrate, none of us is likely to be able to travel abroad."

"That's wild!" Bruce repeated.

We fell silent, looking into the Leningrad night and thinking of my having missed the chance to be born in America.

But did I really miss it? Probably not. I wasn't missing a single thing that I knew of, except for—maybe, vaguely— an opportunity to get to know something that I could miss, like freedom or the green hills of Africa. Freedom was like the taste of avocado: I had never seen an avocado in my life; it could be bad, it could be good, it could have no taste whatsoever. Freedom, for me, was some semblance of inner peace, uninterrupted by fear; no KGB and the borders wide open. I suspected that freedom was a good thing to have, but I never had it; I couldn't miss it. I owed my life only to Russia, which was a disquieting thought. Had my grandmother been taken away to America from Bobruisk, someone else would have been born, in my place and in my time, instead of me. Because my grandfather's parents had never had any intention to emigrate from their Gomel—they were far too poor to be able to afford it—my grandmother would have had to find someone else to marry in America, as would my revolutionary grandfather in Russia; and I, unborn, would have had to rely upon an improbable chance of the properly matched chromosomes. Obviously, I wouldn't be born at all. I owed my life to the unwitting generations of Jews. In order to make me possible, they had worked hard, wandering in the deserts, and then wandering around Europe, and then drifting into Russia one day . . . which was a mistake, I guess . . . and I knew that one day I would drift out of Russia, propelled by curiosity and a general unwillingness to accept that I would never be able to leave the land where I was born. "I would love to emigrate, Bruce," I said.

"Then go for it!" he said. He asked me once whether I wanted to try leaving Russia posing as him, with his passport and ID, which he would claim stolen later on, when I was safely on my way to America. I could barely keep from laughing. Did he think it was so easy to dupe the customs and the border guards, those geniuses of suspicion, those virtuosos of distrust, flicking their shrewd empty eyes from your passport photo to your pale face for as long as it takes you to confess? But even if I succeeded, which I never would—what would happen next? My parents would be harassed by the KGB for years, and I would never see them again. I didn't want that. I needed time. "Forget it, Bruce," I said. He shrugged.

The summer ended. Bruce had safely left my country. We promised to correspond, but we never did. I left my prestigious "mainstream" job and became what I had always wanted to be—a writer, a nightguard, a gas-stoker, a public park attendant, a nobody, a turned-down applicant for an exit visa, a refusenik, a happy man, a serious disappointment to my parents.

(Not that I have always wanted to be a serious disappointment to my parents. Not that my parents are still seriously disappointed in me. Not that our family's story is about disappointment. People are forgiving. Time flies.)

Time did fly, and predictably enough, I grew increasingly set in my uncertain ways. If someone had told me in 1980: "Your plane for the West is leaving in an hour!"—I would have made it to the airport in my last pair of pants. But by 1986, I was full of doubts. I began to realize that I had all I needed to love in my life: my family, my friends, my apartment, my books, my memories. And yet, it was a crazy life, with no future. My friends would die of alcoholism and heart attacks, underground writers would fill their desk drawers with piles upon piles of unpublished stories, and some of us would end up on skid row, wondering if there was something fundamentally wrong with our lives. What is now called in Soviet newspapers the "period of stagnation" was the only life we knew. There is, in fact, a ready metaphor at my fingertips: I once saw, walking around my city, a swallow's nest under the roof of a vacated building scheduled to be torn down, as hundreds of old buildings in downtown Leningrad are. The house looked desolate, depressing, eerie. But the swallow kept cheerily chirping and darting around. Poor bird! I told myself: she just doesn't get it! But then, what else could the bird do? And what else could _we_ do, each of us, me and my friends, going on and on about our lives? The older you get . . . well, the older you get. Already reluctant to leave, I kept applying for an exit visa. OVIR, the regional visa office, would promptly turn me down. Then, on the eve of 1986, suddenly I was permitted to leave. And so I left. When they let you out, you leave. Getting off the bus that took me to the pallid underbelly of the TU-154 plane, silent on a white January tarmac, I turned around and saw a group of my family and friends on the Leningrad International Airport building's concrete balcony a couple of hundred meters away. There was something profoundly mournful about their gathering. They already were my past. Jumping up and down, they desperately waved their hands. Alas, they were waving at the wrong plane. "I'm here!" I shouted, throwing my arms in the air. They couldn't see me. The stewardess gently tapped me on the shoulder. "Come on! It's too late now. Stop making noise," she said. Two hours later I was in Frankfurt. The rest is another story altogether, as my grandmother used to say.

Now, eighty years after the Great Rush to America from within the Pale, I often think about my grandparents, Fyodor Zakharovich Schub and Rakhil Borisovna, or Rachel Borukhovna, Bamm. They are both dead now, and I'm in America.

In 1981, when my grandmother died, my mother sat down and wrote an inspired essay about her mother and gave it to me to read. She was embarrassed, because she felt that writing was not something she could do well, that her writing was some kind of encroachment on my territory. The piece wasn't long—several pages of my grandmother's life condensed. I was very taken by it. One lives, one doesn't write stories like that. Real life is often more literary than the works of literature. That's because it doesn't have to appear credible. Indeed: my grandparents had had a good life together—good only because it was spent together; it was brutally hard, undistinguishable from millions of other Soviet lives. In the end she died of a heart attack on his grave. Things like that never happen in serious novels.

I need not stretch my mind to imagine one more Russian-Jewish emigré family in America, minutes after their ship has brought them to Ellis Island. The year is 1909, or maybe 1910. Standing in the long line of the clerk's desk, they are scared and uncertain, a woman and a man, surrounded by their tired, noisy children. One of their children is my grandmother; she is pretty. She's five and is all wrapped up in a warm black shawl. Everyone's eyes are drawn to ... What should they all be looking at, for the sake of a complete picture? At the Statue of Liberty, I guess, or the Immigration Service clerks. In an hour they're on their own. Now they need a place to settle down in the new world. It will be either Brooklyn or Manhattan. Or maybe Boston. I used to live near Boston.

There's some quiet pleasure in making small symbolic gestures. Now I go to the library at the university where I'm a graduate student. The year is 1988. I pick up the Boston, Brooklyn, and Manhattan phone directories. I know the names I'm looking for. All I can find is a couple of Schubs, a couple of Bamms, and no one with my last name. . . . I expected that. I knew that none of us had ever been in the Abroad before.

Every Hunter
Wants To Know

Every Hunter
Wants to Know

In 1968, when I was thirteen and unhappy, I wrote a story that could have won the prestigious inter–high school literary contest, "Leningrad Teenage Creative Spring." It was called "Kavgolovo" and was about a six year old's first journey into the woods on a mushroom hunt. Our literature teacher had always insisted that writing should be based on personal experience rather than on the power of imagination, and she judged and graded us in accordance with what she perceived as the honesty of our recollections. "Kavgolovo" was an autobiographical story. The reason it didn't win that contest was that shortly before the deadline I changed my mind and submitted another story, "A Fiery Engine," instead. It dealt with a six year old's growing up in Leningrad, his dreamlike childhood memories, his quiet, precocious fascination with the world of words (books!), and an episode of his getting lost—and nearly killed—while marching down Leningrad's main street chanting "We're Number One!" and "We've Made It!" in an exultant crowd celebrating Yuri Gagarin's space flight. Yuri Gagarin was the first man ever to orbit the Earth.

I remember staring at the two stories sitting on the table in front of me. I felt good. By going almost as far back as I could, I seemed to have begun to grapple with the infinite number of my vastly unaccounted for early childhood memories. I also remember being in doubt. "A Fiery Engine" was less autobiographical than "Kavgolovo," but I hoped that our literature teacher would find it more authentic. She knew my family: we were Jewish. Jewish people in Russia usually stay away from the woods.

There are exceptions, of course. One of my grandmothers had always been different. Both she and her older brother, a prominent theoretician in the cellulose industry who drowned swimming in a small northern river in 1968, had always felt out of place in the city. Strong, broad-shouldered, rugged, they were inveterate mushroom gatherers. Neither of them spent much time reading like the rest of our family. Just about the only book I remember my grandmother reading in Kavgolovo (a village near Leningrad) was *The Mushroom Gatherer's Guide*. Published in 1940, it was full of color pictures. I remember looking at them, wondering if a real mushroom looked even half as good. That was a long time ago, in 1961.

The words "mushroom gatherer" *(gribnik)* and "guide, fellow traveller" *(sputnik)* were pitted against one another to form the title in deep red on the blackish cover of my grandmother's book: *Gribnik's Sputnik*. The two words sounded alike, toylike. I couldn't help but associate them with our Soviet Sputnik Number One, that bright, speedy red-hot dot in the sky of 1957, when I was two years old. It could be seen with the naked eye every night that October. But I don't remember actually seeing it then. I remember looking at the sky. I was standing on the kitchen windowsill, my plump feet clasped tightly by two old women from our communal apartment. I strained my eyes in a futile attempt to glimpse the pulsing Sputnik in the sky. Everyone else could see it. "Look, it's right there!" the old women said, pointing. Their heads shook with old age and wonderment. They were almost blind. Everyone was watching, either in the kitchen or in the courtyard six stories below. Our family was in the kitchen, but not my *gribnik* grandmother: it was early October and the woods around Leningrad were still teeming with late mushrooms. Everyone cheered and laughed. One of the hands squeezing my foot was ugly, covered with six furry moles. Slow transparent balloons soared and floated in the sky. Two jars with blackberry preserves sat on the windowsill to the left of my feet. Strings of dried mushrooms dangled above my head. "Can't you see it?" the old women kept saying. "It's right up there, on archangel Gabriel's wing!" They laughed, delighted. "Don't confuse the boy!" my mother said from the darkness behind. The women giggled. Down below, the invisible cheering crowd screamed, stomping their feet, pushing, shoving, squeezing, hugging each other. The air was thick with love. "Sputnik! Sputnik!" someone shouted. That couldn't have been long before a curly-tailed huskie named Laika (or was it Belka, or Strelka?) was shot into space. She never returned. I was three years old and learning how to read. I remember her pug-nosed profile on a soft white and blue pocket-size pack of cheap cigarettes; her name was printed beneath her picture in black letters. I remember wishing I were dead instead of that dog. I envied her fame. She was dead, but famous. She was Number One. The importance that people then attached to one's having done something first—coming in first, dying first—seemed to have deeply impressed me. It was like a deep thirst, this national quest for greatness.

In the summer of the year when smiling Yuri Gagarin was the first man to orbit the Earth, I was six and lived in Kavgolovo, twenty miles from Leningrad. It was a beautiful place. The grandmother-*gribnik* never traveled far away from Leningrad and couldn't stand suburban resorts like Kratovo, a quiet town near Moscow that I don't remember well. I know, however, that we rented a summer house there too, twice. But that's another story altogether. It has nothing to do with mushrooms, or with Gagarin's space flight.

There's a difference between the woods around Moscow and those around Leningrad. The former are less rugged and, like Anton Chekhov, more sadly joyous. Waking up near Moscow, first thing in the morning I would see the green wave of leaves casting uneven shadows on the bedsheets. Tiny, neatly carved, they trembled outside the open window, dripping with fresh green daybreak. Kavgolovo mornings, on the other hand, began with a long branchful of fir needles sharp against the blue sky and solemnly standing like the guards at Lenin's tomb in the Red Square. The moment I woke up I'd forget my dream. Sometimes it would repeat the following night, and then I would recall it, and, of course, forget it again. I developed a habit of screaming in my sleep, rousing myself with a thin wail early in the morning, even if my dream had been good. Everyone in the house would wake up too, shake their heads, and go back to sleep. At one point the doctor had to be consulted. He told my mother that there was nothing wrong with me: unconscious screaming seemed to be my way of coping with growing up. "Sounds fancy," the *gribnik*-grandmother's brother said disapprovingly. For a six year old, I was extremely high-strung.

People lived in every room of the Kavgolovo house: an old unmarried woman who owned it, my mother, my grandmother, her older brother, my toddler brother, and my cousins, Grandmother's brother's two adult sons. My father came down from Leningrad every Sunday (Saturday was still a working day). At night, they all gathered for tea in the living room. The house was full of people. And yet, it was surprisingly silent. Of all the people who were there that summer, I most clearly remember myself.

It was the end of August, days before what is called in Russian "womenfolk's summer"—Indian summer, autumn. Grandmother and her brother had been waiting for rain. They kept looking at the sky, but it was as blue as ever. Then, one morning, the rain began, a sudden shower, full of light; it continued through the afternoon. It was a "mushroom rain": golden threads ran smoothly along the beams of sun. It was, I already knew, a good omen. Russian tradition would expect you to dance barefoot in such a rain. I was sitting in the room I shared with Grandmother, looking out the window at the owner of the house's barking dog, Zhuk, who was four years younger than me. I was six. I knew that everyone expected me, the child, to rush out into the yard, so I decided to stay inside.

"Aren't you bored in there? Come outside!" Grandmother beckoned to me from the yard. She was looking up, smiling. I shook my head, but she wasn't looking at me. The dog kept barking. My mother put aside the magazine she was reading, left the porch and cautiously stepped into the rain. She laughed.

Grandmother's brother, chuckling, walked outside too, stretching and yawning, pretending that he had business to attend to in the yard. My cousins were playing with the dog. The owner of the house brought out two empty buckets to fill with rainwater. Soon everyone was outside. The rain, still benevolently sun-streaked, grew stronger. "Where's Zheka?" my mother asked. Then she saw me in the window and waved. "Come dance with us!" she called. Grandmother turned to her brother and his sons: "Tomorrow? What do you think?" They thought for a moment and seriously nodded their heads.

"Take him with you," my mother said.

Everyone looked up at me. "If he promises not to get lost," Grandmother said.

"Don't scare the boy!" said my mother.

"If he doesn't step on an old German mine and get blown up!" my cousins added, laughing.

"If he doesn't get scared and start screaming and ruin everything," Grandmother's brother said.

"I'm never scared!" I shouted back.

"Well, then, get a good night's sleep," Grandmother told me. Everyone smiled at me. I thought . . . but I don't remember what I thought. Then I thought: "How can one *not* get a good night's sleep?" It was pleasant to be a child and feel smug. I imagined the quiet, giant, slippery mushrooms secretly growing deep in the woods, under wet layers of old pine needles.

It was still early; too early to start thinking about night. There were many long days in each day. The day between dinner and supper was a day. Evening was a day, too. Grandmother would usually go to bed very late.

That Kavgolovo afternoon, 1961, there was a sharp smell of damp hay in the air. Thick light, the color of warm tree sap, poured into the room. The rain dragged on, the yard now empty. I was reading and writing. My room was cozy and austere, like a chronicler's cell: a chair and a table, an open window. Nestor (d.o.b. unknown–died c. 1115), a Russian monk who reputedly wrote the Chronicles of Nestor, must have seen the same serene presunset landscape from his monastery window: docile hills and green grass, smooth under the rain. I had read about him—and seen his picture: long sad nose, a black cassock, a skullcap—in the *Abridged Soviet Encyclopedia* published in 1954. Its three black volumes now sat on the table in front of me, along with the notebook with my name written in angular block letters on the cover and a king-size, lemonade-stained book, *Masterpieces of the Italian Renaissance,* an incomplete collection of black-and-white reproductions. I had the first volume of the encyclopedia opened to the letter "A." With my father's fountain pen, I entered into the notebook the birthdates and deaths of the most prominent people. The fame of each was reflected by the size of the corresponding picture—or its absence. All of them had been involved in some undertaking of the creative spirit and had been known for their progressive ideas. They were revolutionary writers, philosophers, innovative and unorthodox thinkers—the immortals, like Abai Kunanbayev (1845–1904), prominent Kazakh storyteller *(akyn)* and educator, ardent proponent of closer ties between Kazakhstan and Russia; or Khachatur Abovyan (1805–1848), Armenian revolutionary pedagogue and writer; or Martin Andersen-Nekso (b. 1869–still alive as of 1954), a writer of the Danish proletariat. I had been working on "A" for weeks. I was not a fast reader and writer.

I remember feeling good about myself—not just proud because I was the only six year old I knew who had been studying the encyclopedia. Of course, that, too, was important, but I remember thinking that my work had a purpose: to learn the names of all the great people who had ever lived, and to try to find a key to their greatness, or whatever it was that had enabled them to get their names and pictures printed in the encyclopedia. There was a pleasure in counting down the greats, drawing closer to the end of the first letter of the alphabet and—ultimately—to the end of the final volume. It was hard work, too. I wanted all those people sorted out and locked under the cover of my notebook. The dates of their births and deaths, their lives replaced by a short dash seemed to tell me reassuringly: "There's no rush! Relax! You've got all the time in the world!" But, of course, I didn't feel reassured. I didn't have all the time in the world. Time had no meaning whatsoever. Ever since I had learned how to read, I had become more and more frustrated by the sheer abundance of books sitting on the shelves in our Leningrad room. There were hundreds, thousands of them! I remember opening them at random, one by one. Their number seemed infinite. I was keenly aware of the fact that by the time I would be finished with one, there would be thousands of new books added to the number of those already existing in the world. It drove me crazy. How about the fifty-odd volumes of the *Great Soviet Encyclopedia?* How about the complete collection of Leo Tolstoy's works? How about Vladimir Ilyich Lenin's two shelves' worth? I was beginning to suspect that one could easily and forever drown in books and that life was too short for both reading and becoming as great and famous as, for instance, Nestor, who had chosen to write about his life instead of living it, or that poor old Kunanbayev with his goatee. Reading alone, I was afraid, couldn't make one great. What, then, was it good for? I didn't know. If someone had asked me if I'd rather be alive, knowing I'd never get into the encyclopedia, or die now and immediately be made immortally famous, I wouldn't hesitate to make my choice. And yet, it had already crossed my mind that the time would come when I would realize that the dead are always at a disadvantage.

Soon I got tired and put down the pen. The rain had stopped—and changed the view from my window. I started daydreaming. The empty yard, encircled by a black picket fence where an angry Kavgolovo raven grimly perched, gave way to a ravine. The wind was warm. Lamblike clouds, reflected in the silver river, moved across the timeless sky with considerable speed. Clusters of trees were scattered over the green hills. I was not imagining them. Imagining things was a waste of time. I was in my Kavgolovo room, looking at a picture in a book on the table in front of me. Then I looked up again. The view perfectly matched one of the reproductions from the *Masterpieces of the Italian Renaissance*—a heavy tome with the many pictures of naked men and women missing (Grandmother must have ripped them out)—namely, "The Old Man and His Grandson," by Domenico Ghirlandajo. In the background, behind the faces of an old man and a young boy, was a ravine and a silver snake of a river. Medieval Italy looked amazingly like Kavgolovo.

Whenever I opened that book, touching with my fingers the remaining fragile pages that were carefully separated by rustling rice paper, it occurred to me that I might be the only six year old in Kavgolovo who was enjoying the masterpieces of the Italian Renaissance. Time stood still and it seemed to me that I had existed forever. I leaned down to the small print in the parentheses to see how old Ghirlandajo (Domenico Di Tommaso Bigordi) was at the time of his death. Only forty-five! I was unnerved. 1449–1494: it was amusing that his life boiled down to a matter of inverted digits. It ended with the last two digits of the year of his birth, reversed. This could never happen to me. I was born in 1955. I was lucky.

That picture was a quiet joy to behold. The Renaissance old man resembled my grandfather: his nose was bulbous and his eyes seemed just as ready to well up with teary emotion. My grandfather was still alive. Five hundred years ago there was no Leningrad, no Lenin. The old man's grandson was my age, but he had been dead for the last five hundred years. Looking at that picture made me sleepy. I lay down on my bed and fell asleep, and my dream was pleasant. Then someone tapped me on the shoulder. I stretched and smiled, a child rising to the surface of his dream, and opened my eyes.

It was dark. Grandmother was standing over my bed. An enormous wicker basket with the mushroom knife rolling loudly across its bottom dangled from her elbow. "What time is it?" I asked. She said: "Three." I got up. She made me pull on two pairs of pants, knee-high rubber boots that an adder couldn't bite through, and a *budyonovka*, a flannel, pointed helmet with flapping ears named after the founder of the Red Cavalry, Semyon Mikhailovich Budenny, a silly-looking headpiece to protect my hair against ticks, the carriers of encephalitis. We walked outside. Grandmother's brother and his sons were waiting in the yard, their faces serious. Zhuk, the dog, squealed thinly. The mist smelled of cold earth, worms, and fish. Grandmother took me by the hand and we set out for the woods. We went in silence. Then she looked at me and said: "Come on! Aren't you excited? Today's your big day!"

"Yes, yes, I'm excited!" I said, stifling a smile. Everyone seemed pleased with my answer. We walked along the railroad tracks, empty and stained with smelly grease. The woods on both sides of the tracks were two gray walls of trees. I had never been up that early—or that late. No other six year old could possibly be awake at this hour. After a while, we turned right and entered the woods.

Surprisingly, the woods were not as dark as the open space, but the infinity of the trees was overwhelming. They couldn't be counted, and even if I had spent the rest of my life here, I still wouldn't be able to touch the bark of each. There were just too many of them. Soon, after grandmother had released my hand and everyone had wandered off and coalesced with the shadows of the trees, I got lost and found myself standing in front of a tall fir tree, staring at two mushrooms. I identified them as orange caps, or *podosinoviki*. They looked exactly like their pictures in the *Mushroom Gatherer's Guide*. "Not bad!" I thought. "But what do I do next?" I knew, of course, how I should feel, being so

much closer to the beginning of my life than to its end—as
a natural part of nature which has no memory and survives
by instinct: like a mushroom, a plant, or a grassblade. I
was on my own in the woods. I smiled and hollered, but
my voice sounded unconvincing and hollow. "I feel good!"
I told myself, but I felt a little uneasy. Suddenly I knew
that I had stood in this spot before. But when? I looked
around. It was getting light. The moss under my feet was
streaked by the sun. It was dry, despite the recent rain.
Something rustled behind my back: a hare or a fox, or a
snake. Birds were beginning to test their voices overhead.
To my left was a thick aspen, a treacherous Judas of Russian trees, covered with black spots like a hyena. Its minute
leaves shivered as though in fever. On its mossy lee side
had to be a *chaga* outgrowth, a dark gray porous fungus—
touchwood. According to the *Mushroom Gatherer's Guide*,
drinking its extract could help one suffering from cancer
survive. I squinted, peering through the dusk. There it was,
chaga, a hundred years old. I stepped over to the tree and
saw it. It seemed wet. I touched it. It was wet. Then I
remembered that *chaga* was also called birch tree sponge—
beryozovaya gubka—and that it didn't grow on aspens. I took
another look at the tree and saw that I had been mistaken.
It was a birch, the dear soul of Russia. When I touched it,
its bark felt like onion peels. A sudden gust of wind set its
leaves in motion. Then everything settled back into silence.
I didn't know how much time had passed. It didn't really
matter. Time had no meaning; not yet. Every minute for
me was ten times longer than for my grandmother, and she
was nowhere to be seen. I yanked the mushrooms from the
moss and squeezed them to my chest. They were heavy.
"I'm here!" I called loudly. No one answered. The sun kept
rising and its light was familiar. "I have been here before!"
I thought, frightened by the strangeness of recognition. It
occurred to me then that maybe I was living someone else's

life, which had already ended—and maybe (this made more sense) I was remembering things from my own future: that would explain why, finding myself lost in the woods, I kept doing the same thing every time, over and over again— running around in circles with my heart beating louder than the crackling of frail twigs under my feet or the warbling of wild birds overhead. I knew that this thought was too sophisticated for a six year old. I screamed tentatively. My voice boomed in silence; it boomeranged. Filled with my panting, the silence was no longer complete. I bolted. The forest darkened; I was breathing too deep, too fast. "Don't panic!" I shouted. The birds in the tree branches were full of indifference. I ran forever. Once or twice my foot slipped through windows of dangerous, deep mud thinly veiled by bright patches of decaying leaves. When, screaming, I jerked my foot out, the dirt gave with a greedy sigh and the greasy smacking of fat, disappointed lips. Soon, having completed a full circle, which could only mean that my right foot was stronger than the left one, I returned to the place where I had found the mushrooms. Then, too tired to scream, I remembered that real *gribniks,* so as not to scare away the mushrooms, communicated with each other by way of cautious hallooing. It was too late for me, though. I was lost for good.

"Halloo!" I hollered, and heard a dog's barking, and then a sweet and close "halloo" in response. A dog—it was Zhuk—cheerfully jumped at me from behind the nearest tree. Grandmother stepped out of the shadows. She stopped in front of two fresh black wounds in the moss. "Someone's beat us to two mushrooms!" she said angrily.

She didn't notice that I had been lost, which meant that I hadn't been lost. "Scared?" she asked, and I realized that she had been keeping an eye on me all along. She glanced

at me and smiled. "You did all the right things," she said
approvingly. "You were smart to start screaming. You didn't
have to run, though. It always makes things worse. Next
time stay right where you are and keep screaming."

"I knew I wasn't lost," I said sheepishly. "I was just
teasing you."

She smiled again. I remembered the mushrooms that
I had found. Running around, I had dropped one of them. I
showed her the one that I still clutched to my chest. Her
face brightened.

"Congratulations! Now you're a *gribnik!*" she said. Then
her face took on a stern expression: "Don't you know you
should have used the knife? Now you've destroyed the roots
and there won't be any new mushrooms here next year!"

"But I don't have a knife!" I said.

She shook her head: "You should've called for me. I
would've come over with my knife!" She grabbed my hand
and slapped it. I started to cry. She hugged me. "I'm sorry,
I'm sorry!" she said.

Her basket was full. There were all kinds of mushrooms inside. It was a shame, I thought, to leave so many
mushrooms behind, in the woods, just because there was
no more room in her basket. But we had to go. I was still
looking around, remembering. On the way out of the woods,
I spotted a colony of *lisichki*, or "little foxes," with their
brilliant yellow cups, and an assorted bunch of gilled, pink
and red and yellow *syroyezhki*, which can be eaten raw, as
their name in Russian implies (of course, no one eats them
raw). Later I saw a pale death cap, the destroying angel,
more poisonous than cyanide and more lethal than the fancy
scarlet, white-dotted fly killer—*mukhomor*. Redheaded
podosinoviki grew under the aspens; prim *podberyozoviki*
sprouted under the birch trees. The diminutive slippery
jacks—*maslyata*, or "the buttery ones"—were covered with
slimy film. "White mushrooms," or *boroviki*, were the kings

of mushrooms. Grandmother would hang them on a thread over the stove to dry.

The woods were abundant with mushrooms that morning. It was sad to leave them all behind, unaccounted for. Indeed, if all I could do was to remember seeing them in the woods, I could just as well have imagined them, and then convinced myself, as I have often done since, that imagination is the best and most reliable source of recollections. I could have stayed home, waiting for Grandmother, for her brother with his sons, and for the dog to appear in our yard with their baskets full of the Kavgolovo mushrooms. At times I even seem to remember standing next to my mother in the yard of the Kavgolovo house that morning, looking at the *gribniks* and exclaiming: "At last! How was it, granny? What took you so long? Why didn't you take me with you? Why didn't you wake me up?" Maybe I wasn't in the woods with my grandmother, after all. That was such a long time ago. Yet I clearly remember being there with her.

We all gathered together at the edge of the forest, the five of us—but the dog, Zhuk, was nowhere to be seen. "Zhuk! Zhuk!" I called out twice. Grandmother, radiant after a good mushroom hunt, hugged me and said: "Don't you cry, he'll be back! He's just a dog!" I wasn't about to cry, until she said it. Then tears appeared in my eyes. I turned away. She paid no attention to me.

"Zheka's found a huge mushroom!" she said.

Her brother and his sons nodded, wasting no words. They, too, were proud of me.

"Big deal!" one of my cousins said.

"I found *two* mushrooms!" I corrected Grandmother.

"Of course," she said.

Their baskets were full of mushrooms covered with fresh leaves, green needles, and ferns in order to protect them from the rising sun and from the stares and questions of

other mushroom gatherers along the way. It was considered bad luck and bad taste to reveal one's mushroom-
picking spots. On our way back, Grandmother suggested
that we take the picturesque lakeside road. I wanted to stay
and wait for the dog, but Grandmother, or maybe it was
her brother, told me that he must have run into some of his
friends back there in the woods. "What friends?" I thought.
I hated it when grown-ups talked to me condescendingly.

"What friends? Are you out of your mind?" I said.

"Dog hunters," my cousins said, laughing, expecting me
to start crying.

"Stop teasing him!" Grandmother said.

I began to weep softly.

"He's very tired," Grandmother said. "Let's go home."

They patted my head, but I kept crying. "Shut up!"
Grandmother's brother said sternly, giving me an excuse
to become confused and inconsolable. Tears were sweet.
They had a life of their own. Overtaken by the mysterious
process of dissolving into tears, I forgot the cause and purpose of my despair. I gagged and choked. Grandmother's
brother picked me up and set me down on his shoulders.
"Look, he's smiling through his tears, like Chekhov!"
Grandmother said.

"What a pain!" one of my cousins said.

I smiled.

We walked down the green hills that Kavgolovo is so famous
for, past the serene and blue Kavgolovo lake. The weather
was good. Gently swaying brown pines and firs climbed up
the hills that looked like an Italian picture. High in the sky,
two slender white scars in the wake of two invisible planes
grew rapidly and stretched across the deep blue altitude.
They were the color of early morning snow outside the ice-
bitten window of the tourist center, a log cabin with two

rooms and two windows, not far from Leningrad.

That was a long time ago, before I started to scream waking up. It was January, or December. I awoke and looked around, feeling cold, and saw my mother sleeping in the bed across the room, her pink toes peeking out from under the maize-colored woolen blanket with the purple ink stamp of the tourist center. I considered falling back asleep and decided against it. Nothing was happening, nothing was going to happen. Once started, the day could neither stop nor end. Minutes passed. There was a brick stove in the far corner of the room. It was cold. Loud snoring came from another room. I was three, or two.

Now the forest, the Kavgolovo lake, and the sky, healed from the planes' invasion, were crisp and clear. I shuddered with the anticipation of memories to come; there was a firm and conclusive promise in my having been able, at age six, to recall what had happened to me three, or even four years before. I already had, at age six, a solid stock of memories to draw upon! I smiled at the thought that when I was ten or twenty I would have so many memories that I would be able to do nothing but reminisce, pondering and comparing the events of my life against one other.

Then we came close to our house. Grandmother's brother unsaddled me from his shoulders.

My mother was waiting for us in the yard. "At last!" she exclaimed. "How was it? What took you so long?" I told her that we had lost the dog. "He'll be back," she said. We put our baskets up on the table and began to sort the mushrooms, arranging them in separate piles on the newspaper that was spread out across the tabletop. "Let me do this!" I said. "Let me count them!" They stepped aside from the table and began to watch me. I was good with numbers.

It turned out that we had gathered 34 *syroyezhki;* 178 *lisichki*, already wilting and crumbling in their fragile yellow beauty; 102 *maslyata*, or slippery jacks; 52 *podberyozo-*

viki; 40 *podosinoviki,* good for pickling, their red caps clasping rough and rugged gray-streaked stems so tight that they looked like giant matches waiting to be struck; and 47 *boroviki.* It had been a great mushroom hunt.

When the baskets finally were empty, I felt disappointed, as though I had hoped to find something exceptional at the bottom of each. I had no idea what I was looking for: maybe a surprisingly huge, ugly mushroom, or a very tiny one. I stepped back from the table and wiped my hands on the front of my red checkered flannel shirt.

"This boy is destined to become a mathematician!" Grandmother said.

My mother nodded. "Remember when he used to spend hours by the highway?"

"Oh yes." Grandmother smiled. "Maybe you should send him to a special school for gifted children."

"Don't confuse the boy," said my mother.

They were recalling the summer before in Komarovo, near Leningrad, when I used to spend hours by the highway, counting the cars that sped by. There were few of them, headed toward Leningrad or—much less frequently—from Leningrad toward northern Karelia and the state border of another country. The cars were slick and mesmerizing, each unexpected, appearing out of nowhere. I counted them, though I wasn't interested in the total number as such. All I really wanted to know was that the total was finite. In one hour, twenty-five Pobedas went by, ten new Volgas, eight posh, raven-black ZIMs, and twenty old Moskviches. I paid no attention to trucks and vans. To sort them out and keep their respective quantities in mind was interesting, but less important than the hope of being able, provided I stayed right there by the highway long enough, to count all the cars in Leningrad, or in Karelia, or even in the entire Soviet Union. I knew that it probably couldn't be done, but I had a feeling that maybe it could. And of course, I was looking for something surprising and unusual. That was what kept me there in the first place. I wanted to witness something unexpected, like a foreign car on the road (Finland was not far away), or maybe a horsecart, or a car accident. That same anxious feeling of standing on the verge of a surprise propelled me through the pages of the encyclopedia in my Kavgolovo room. I knew that I might discover on the next page that some writer had lived for almost two hundred years. It was highly unlikely, but it could happen. And there was a sense of doing a job, too. The more I read and counted, and kept the faces and numbers in my mind, the closer I was to the end, and being closer to the end was a good feeling. That feeling was decidedly unmathematical and defied any attempt at common-sense calculation. I simply wanted to see the end of the book, the emptiness of the road. There were only so many cars in the country; only so many mushrooms in the woods; only so many people in the world; only so many famous names in the encyclopedia. I could talk with every man alive. In the end, I could get to know them all. I flipped through the pages, and if one was worth no more attention than the next, I sighed with relief: I was drawing closer to the end. In the end, I would do all right. I would survive.

After dinner, when the rain began again and everyone in the house was sleeping, I stepped out into the yard. The rain grew stronger and colder. Remembering that it was my birthday, I ran around the yard, filled with excitement, sloshing in the puddles, repeating my age—"Six-six-six"— until the words lost their meaning and fell into the black depths of the language. I liked to play with words that I knew, repeating them until they began to sound funny, then scary. "Mother-mother-mother," I would repeat rapidly. "Blue. Blue-blue-blue. House-house-house"—and in no time at all the word would be menacingly transformed into something new: what was "mothermo?" What color was "blueb?" "Househou?" Each time, the sudden disappearance of the word's meaning scared me: where did it go? When I stopped running around, I remembered that it was, of course, *not* my birthday. My birthday was in July, and there are almost no mushrooms in the woods until late August. I was already six. I stopped and paused. A cheering crowd approached our house. People were dancing, laughing, and screaming. Yuri Levitan in his deep, sonorous voice that was used only for radio news of planetary importance was announcing the triumph of Soviet spirit and science. "His name is Yuri Alexeyevich Gagarin, he is twenty-seven years old!" he exclaimed. The crowd went berserk. Never before had I witnessed such undiluted joy, such selfless exhilaration, such shameless happiness. People beckoned to me. I made a timid step forward, toward another story, "A Fiery Engine."

Then it occurred to me that Yuri Gagarin was launched into orbit on April 12, 1961, not in August. The dancing and cheering crowd, chanting "We've Made It!" and "We're Number One!" might instead be celebrating Space Flight Number Two in August of 1961—but, of course, I wouldn't remember it. Number Two didn't count. It's the first time, no matter what, that is always memorable. In my mind, I was back in Leningrad. Yuri Gagarin had been launched into space.

The crowds cheered. Everywhere—in Moscow, in Leningrad—people rejoiced and took to the streets. As happy as if someone had promised to keep them alive forever, they were carrying huge pictures of Yuri Gagarin's typically Russian face—so fit for print in the *Encyclopedia*—with its multi-dimpled, frozen smile: it floated slowly through the pink air of April.

That day, April 12, 1961, so many euphoric people were in the streets that some of them got stomped and trod upon, crushed and squashed under hundreds of feet. There were casualties, just like in 1953, when Stalin died and crowds gathered in their immeasurable grief. I remember thinking that those who were killed in the mourning crowd passed away at the very depth of unhappiness, their eyes full of tears and their hearts filled with boundless sorrow. They stumbled and staggered along, and then they went down, still crying, unable to see anything, falling smoothly through one darkness into another, more permanent. But those who were squeezed to death in the happy crowd of Gagarin's great victory were happier than they were ever likely to be if they had had a chance to keep on living. They shouted and chanted at the top of their lungs, too excited to notice their own deaths. The song that they sang played on the radio day and night. It went like this:

We all were born to make the legend real!
To claim the space! To work and study hard!
Our mind has given us strong wings of steel!
A fiery engine to replace the heart!

In 1961, Gagarin himself had no more than seven years to live. The plane he piloted lost altitude and crashed into a Russian forest. That was in 1968. He was thirty-four. I was thirteen and in high school.

The news of his death was announced on the radio the next day, after I had left for school. Our literature teacher entered the class sobbing. By sheer coincidence, it was the same day that my story, "A Fiery Engine," was to be proclaimed a winner in the inter–high school competition. I already knew that it had won. It was supposed to be a big day for me. It was also the hundredth anniversary of the birth of Maxim Gorky, the most famous Soviet writer of all time, March 28. I remember thinking how symbolic it would be to have my literary career launched on the hundredth anniversary of his death.

Instead of congratulating me and inviting the class to give me a round of applause, as she had promised me she'd do, the teacher sighed deeply and said: "I want you all to stand up. I have devastating news. Yuri Alexeyevich Gagarin is dead!"

There was a pause. We didn't know what to say, how to mourn. Class was promptly dismissed. We poured out, laughing, full of plans. I was disappointed and sad that Gagarin's death had so crudely intervened with my own life. However, by that time he was no longer Number One, and I was no longer six years old, and I didn't wish that I was dead instead.

But back in 1961, all that was still a lifetime away. I was in Kavgolovo. The rain had stopped and, sure enough, there was a rainbow in the sky. I looked at it for some time. Its colors were: red, then orange, yellow, green, blue, indigo, and violet. This sequence was easy to remember once you memorized the sentence in which the first letter of each word was the first letter of one of the rainbow's colors: "Kazhdyi Okhotnik Zhelayet Znat Gdye Skryvayetsya Fazan": Every Hunter Wants To Know Where the Pheasant's Hiding. I always wondered who had come up with this idea first.

It was the hour of the day when the sun strikes the eye at a crimson angle and everything begins to look eerily intense, but serene: a late August afternoon the color of an April evening. I was in my room, watching. The trees and the hills were green, there were swallows in the sky, and Russia was joyous and looked eternal beyond my window.

Late at night, unable to fall asleep, I stepped out of my room and walked to the kitchen. There was a thick thread of drying mushrooms stretched over the stove. The stove was hot, the coals were still burning inside. To get perfectly dry mushrooms, an indispensable vitamin source during the winter, Grandmother would keep them hanging over the stove for several weeks.

I reached out and touched one mushroom with my fingers. Still wet, it was already shriveled. I squeezed it hard, imagining everyone's surprise next morning, when they discovered that one mushroom on the thread of forty-seven *boroviki* was prematurely perfectly dry and ready to cook. Drops of bitter-smelling mushroom juice fell on the oven. There was a loud hissing; a cloud of dark bitterness hit my nostrils. When I dropped the mushroom, my index finger brushed against the metallic oven top. I was more scared than hurt. I knew that everyone would wake up if I screamed, but I couldn't help it. I had no other recourse. I remember screaming. That was a long time ago.

Red Square

Early in the morning one March, at the end of the sixth winter of his life, a Leningrad boy named Yevgeny—Zheka, for short—was sitting at his grandparents' breakfast table in Losinoostrovskaya, or Moose Island, a town on the outskirts of Moscow. Still half asleep because of the pain that had kept him up most of the night, he was gazing out the ground-floor window, listening to the *Pioneers' Dawn* program on the radio as the First Moscow Boys Choir sang "We Think of *Him* on the Forty-Fourth Year of Our Revolution!" His *Leningrad Kindergartner* textbook, open to a large black-and-white picture of two Young Pioneer Heroes being executed by a German firing squad, was propped against a souvenir electric samovar on the table. Zheka was waiting for Grandfather to return from Leningrad.

Zheka's grandmother was in the kitchen. She stood beside the gas stove in the warm glow of a yellow lightbulb overhead, stirring oatmeal kasha. When it began to bubble, she poured it out onto a steaming plate and set it down before Zheka.

"Stop staring at that book! Eat! Open your mouth!" she said in a stern voice. He realized that she, too, was still upset by the news of old Seraphima's death.

A spoon of hot cereal trembled in her hand one centimeter from his lips.

He averted his face.

"I'm in no mood for playing games today!" she said.

"Are you mad at me?" he asked. "Why? What did I do?"

It occurred to him that she had forgotten to give him his white painkilling pill.

Zheka's mouth felt especially raw today. His lower jaw and the entire right side of his face were severely infected.

A month ago he had become allergic to something in the Losinoostrovskaya water. In order to prevent the disease from spreading, a number of his teeth had been extracted. He'd been checked into the district hospital during a feverish bout of seizures, after a series of Grandfather's midnight calls to the emergency room. Zheka's grandfather was an old bolshevik, vice-chairman of the local chapter of the Old Bolsheviks' Union. He was entitled to one of the few private telephones in Losinoostrovskaya.

Zheka could no longer eat cold or solid food, or drink anything that hadn't been boiled first.

He hated being helpless.

One of his frequent thoughts was that nothing nearly as bad would have happened to him if only his mother— his grandparents' daughter, their only child—had let him stay in Leningrad.

True, Leningrad water was unhealthy and dirty, or so they said, but he had been drinking it since birth.

"What about me? I could die too!" he'd said to his mother during the most recent of their weekly telephone conversations. She had just told him that Seraphima, an insane woman who used to live in one of the rooms of their apartment, had gone to bed one night and never woke up again.

"Who's talking about death?" his mother said. "She's not dead. She's asleep, that's all. Now listen, your little brother wants to tell you something!" Zheka listened to an ear-piercing, piggish shriek.

"Asleep!" he thought. "Who does she think I am?" He hung up. That was three days ago.

Zheka had gone to live with his grandparents last fall, after his mother had a second son.

Zheka's father was a scientist and needed peace and quiet. He was spending the nights at the public library.

Zheka remembered his father tiptoeing back into their room early in the morning, when most of their sixteen communal apartment neighbors had already left for work. Those were not the best of times. His mother and father either argued in a furious whisper out in the corridor or silently avoided each other's eyes. The baby, Zheka's brother, screamed at the top of its lungs.

Their single-family room had become too small for four people.

On the other hand, here, in Losinoostrovskaya, the air was always still.

"I don't have all day!" Grandmother said.

At that moment Zheka's thoughts were interrupted by the startling ring of their telephone in the family room.

He and Grandmother looked at each other. She dropped the spoon and hurried out of the kitchen. Zheka followed her into the family room. The Kremlin Courants began to strike eight o'clock on the kitchen radio. Grandmother lifted the receiver.

"Yes. Speak up!" she said, a little short of breath. There was silence.

Then her face fell.

"I knew you were absolutely helpless," she said. "Poor girl: to have a father like you and a husband like him! You were supposed to try and talk some sense into his head! Did you tell him that I'm writing a letter about his behavior to his Party Committee? That'll serve him right!" She hung up.

"I'm so tired!" she said to Zheka.

Zheka nodded.

"Who was it?" he asked.

"Your Granddaddy," Grandmother said, looking out the window. "He's back in Moscow, at the train station."

"Did he say anything about Seraphima?" Zheka asked. "Is she still dead?"

"Oh, for Christ's sake!" she exclaimed. "Leave me alone!"

"Christ is neither here nor there," Zheka said. They returned to the kitchen.

It was already light outside the kitchen window. A short pause on the radio was followed by the eight o'clock news with Yuri Levitan. He cleared his throat and began reciting the daily list of ordinary citizens who had sent their telegrams thanking Uncle Nikita for his firmness in dealing with Adenauer and Eisenhower during his recent trip abroad. Then someone else solemnly declaimed the Supreme Soviet's letter to the leaders of Freedom-Fighting African Nations.

Grandmother picked up the spoon from the table and tasted the kasha with the tip of her tongue.

Zheka climbed back into his chair, still listening. The African names were as weightless as bits of fish food floating in a fish tank.

"Lumumba!" Zheka said loudly. "They killed him! Do you know what Tshombe's men did to him? They put an automobile tire around his neck and set it on fire!"

"I want you to eat your breakfast!" Grandmother said.

"I don't understand your fascination with cruelty. Give me that book!"

With her free hand, she tried to grab his textbook. Zheka hid the book behind his back.

"Patrice Lumumba!" he shouted. "Moice Tshombe! Kill Tshombe! America!"

Grandmother shook her head.

"Down with America!" Zheka thought.

He felt excited.

In the kindergarten yard in Leningrad, he and his classmates used to play the Red Cavalry game. Some of the boys, the most awkward and least respected, were the enemy. Their frightened army was called America. Zheka's cavalry, led by the legendary marshals Budenny and Voroshilov, each time effortlessly scattered their lines of defense.

"Down with America!" roared the Red Cavalry, swinging their toy sabers above their heads.

A hot wave of ardor swelled in Zheka's chest.

He yawned. Grandmother immediately guided the spoon into his open mouth.

"Now-now-now," she said. "I know it's still hot, I know you don't like it, but it's good for you!"

He gagged and shook his head.

"Look!" she said. "This plate is a train, and you're an engineer! This spoon is one of the train's cars. Your mother's in this car. This one's your little brother's. This one's your Granddaddy's. And this one—guess what?—is *me*. Now you have all your loved ones in your tummy!"

That was the game they played every morning.

Grandmother was no longer upset.

After breakfast, Zheka walked to the kitchen window and watched the snow begin to fall outside.

Lately it had been warm.

This spring weather was unpredictable.

Snow covered the trees lining the street. Black birds perched on their gnarled branches, reminding Zheka of rooks from Savrasov's painting "Rooks Are Back" in the "Our Soviet Spring" section of his kindergarten textbook.

One of the birds suddenly took to the air and disappeared from view.

An old rusted Pobeda, the first postwar national car, whooshed by, enveloped in a cloud of snow-colored exhaust. A white horse dragged a squeaking wooden cart down the street.

Zheka pressed his nose to the chilly windowpane. Faint smoke rose above the roofs both nearby and off in the distance. A drunk old man ambled along the street and shouted something in response to his wife's booming admonitions. Remote, discordant singing could be heard on the outskirts of town. Voices, loud laughter, dogs barking, a child wailing, shreds of words Zheka couldn't understand, the rhythmic sound of drums or tambourines soon vanished back into the silence of the snowfall.

Zheka picked up his textbook from his chair and went into the family room. There he sat at Grandfather's desk and wrote in block letters on a clean sheet of paper: "My dear! I'm fine! How are you? I'm being good!"

Those were the only words Grandfather had taught him to write.

Zheka could think of nothing more to say today anyway. He sat on the floor and looked at the carpet hanging on the wall. It was a reproduction of the cast-iron fence of the Summer Garden in Leningrad.

According to a footnote in the "Be Proud of Your City" section of Zheka's textbook, that fence was so beautiful that terminally ill people from all over the world were coming to Leningrad to see it. One was considered lucky to have died near the Summer Garden's fence.

Zheka winced at the worsening pain in his mouth and prepared to sing.

He closed his eyes and imagined his listeners' attentive faces hanging out of every window.

Zheka sang so much and so well that Grandfather even took him once to the First Moscow Boys Choir audition in downtown Moscow, near Red Square, where everyone loved his voice. The only reason the choir didn't accept him then was his age. All the other boys in the choir were seven or eight years old.

Zheka would have to wait.

He opened his eyes and saw that it was still snowing outside. Thick clumps of wet snow fell slantwise across the space between sky and earth.

Zheka could tell that it was for the last time this winter that the drafty air would smell of cold apples.

He started singing one of his favorite songs, "Beyond the Factory Walls."

It was about the life and death of a curly-haired boy who was born at the beginning of the century, either in Moscow or in Leningrad, or Petersburg.

"The tree blossoms were thick in the air beyond the Factory Walls," Zheka sang. "Hungry, cold, there lived a boy with curly hair. He was seventeen years old. After the Great Day in October the boy was free and happy at last! The time of the capitalists was over! But they kept clinging to the past!"

Zheka had read about the war between the Reds and the Whites in the "Our First Years" section of his textbook.

He hated the Whites.

"That was a long time ago. The boy wanted to live, because—he was young! But he decided to go off to war for the working class's cause!"

Zheka's voice soared to the ceiling.

The enemy bullet pierced the boy's heart. His shirt,

soaked with blood, was like a banner of the Revolution!

"Do me a favor, stop screaming!" Grandmother said, walking in from the kitchen.

Zheka fell silent, filled with quiet grief. He, too, wanted to be sung about!

"Do something!" Grandmother said. "Take a nap!"

"I don't want to sleep!" Zheka said.

He had a very strong headache.

Grandmother returned to the kitchen.

Zheka drew in air and shouted the beginning of another song: "Yes, friends! Yes! It's in our power to save the planet from nuclear war!"

"Shut up!" Grandmother yelled at him from behind the wall.

Suddenly feeling sad, Zheka stopped singing.

"Where is he?" he thought.

Indeed, how long could it take Grandfather to get home from the train station?

Zheka had nothing else to do but start thinking about Seraphima again.

He remembered, for the hundredth time in the last three days, her startled face as he, Tolyan, and Yulka burst into her room.

Tolyan and Yulka also lived in the old communal apartment. They were Zheka's age.

They'd scared Seraphima to death!

She believed in God. The walls in her room were hung with dark icons.

Late at night, she shuffled along the corridor, with a lit candle in her hand.

She saw visions of the Archangel Gabriel.

The Angel of Death spoke with her.

She was crazy.

When Zheka had told his kindergarten teacher that one of the women in his apartment believed in God, she suggested that he read to Seraphima aloud from the "Old People's Superstitions and How To Fight Them" section of his textbook.

Zheka didn't like the idea.

"Boring!" he thought.

The next morning Zheka, Yulka, and Tolyan put white sheets over their heads and stomped into Seraphima's room.

"I'm the Archangel Gabriel!" Zheka hollered from the door. "Your time has come, Seraphima! Prepare to die!"

He walked to the wall and yanked down one of the icons. It was heavy.

Seraphima sucked in air and crossed herself.

Tolyan laughed and gave her a slight push in the back.

She fell to the floor.

Zheka reached with his index finger into his mouth and touched the right side of his lower jaw: his gum was swollen and inflamed.

He got up off the floor and lay down on the couch in the corner. The smell of varnish and dust began to put him to sleep. He turned on his side and drew his knees up to his chest.

Once again, he heard footsteps outside.

They drew nearer.

He fell asleep.

Someone knocked on the front door, then rang the doorbell.

He thought at first that the ringing was the continuation of the loud, endless whistle of a boiling teakettle in his dream. He waited, shivering with cold.

The sound, shrill and urgent, was repeated.

"Grandfather's lost his keys!" he thought.

He jumped off the couch and ran into the hallway. The light there was dim. Grandmother, wiping her hands on her apron, stood a step away from the door.

"Who's there?" she asked in a firm voice.

"Let me in, dear woman!" came a plaintive female voice murmuring from the other side of the door. "Please, let me call the hospital! I'm told you have a telephone! My baby son is dying of pneumonia!"

The woman began to sob.

"I don't know," Grandmother said. "This is very unusual. How can I be sure you're telling me the truth? I need to see your identification papers."

There was no response.

"Well, then," Grandmother said, shrugging. "I can't let you in."

She turned to leave.

Zheka, surprised by his own boldness, grabbed her sleeve.

"Her *son* is dying!" he exclaimed.

Grandmother's face reddened with embarrassment!

"Go back to the family room! You're too small to understand!" she whispered. "There are so many crooks and criminals wandering around these days, thanks to that profound thinker Nikita and his amnesty!"

She waved Zheka away.

Zheka didn't like it that she seemed to be talking about Uncle Nikita in a disapproving way. It reminded him of his father in front of the TV in their room in Leningrad, chuckling and saying things that made Zheka regret being his son. He didn't know the meaning of the word "crooks," but he assumed they were the same people who recently, until the Losinoostrovskaya militia finally caught them, had been placing threatening notes under people's doormats: "Please, be so kind as to put an envelope with five hundred rubles under this same doormat by 6 A.M. tomorrow. Otherwise we'll have to slit your throat. Best wishes, Eisenhower and Adenauer."

"I understand everything!" Zheka said. "Let her in!"

The woman on the other side of the door let out a wail of despair.

Grandmother reluctantly unlocked the door. "Come on in," she said. "Let's get it over with!"

The door swung open at once. A crowd of bearded men and black-shawled, black-haired women in flowing gaudy clothes streamed into the apartment. They were enveloped in a cloud of oily-smelling perfume. The men played their guitars and banged on tight-skinned gongs. The women waved their hands above their heads, singing and talking rapidly in a strange language.

The jangling of their necklaces of small coins filled Zheka's soul with joy.

The gypsies danced their way into the kitchen, into the family room, into Zheka's grandparents' bedroom.

They seemed happy.

"Show me your palm!" shouted one woman in a flowered shawl, hugging Grandmother.

"Spare some change!" begged another.

Grandmother screamed, opening her mouth wide.

Zheka could barely hear her.

A tall man lifted him off the floor and held him up to the ceiling.

"A boy! A boy!" someone said.

"What wonderful curly hair! What an angel!" someone else breathed out.

Zheka closed his eyes.

"Are you going to be a pilot when you grow up?" the man asked.

"I don't know," Zheka said. "I can sing!"

The man smiled.

"Is that so?" he said. "That's good. We need singing boys!"

He lowered Zheka down and turned to a young and

beautiful gypsy woman standing next to him. "He's yours!" he said.

She took Zheka's hand and headed out the front door.

Bright light made him screw his eyes shut for a moment.

They walked across the porous snow in silence. Zheka's slippered feet soon became hopelessly wet. The pain lodged inside his jaw close by his right ear began to stir again. He couldn't tell how much time had passed.

Zheka looked around him.

Grandmother, a fur coat thrown over her shoulders, ran down the steps of the stoop. Breathing heavily, she struck him across the face.

Zheka began to cry.

"I'm sorry, I'm sorry! It's just that you scared me so much!" she said.

They waded through the snow back home.

Zheka's mouth was hurting.

It was hard to imagine the pain ever going away.

When Zheka awoke, it was already afternoon. Grandfather was home. "Look, if this is what you think we should do, let's do it," he said to Grandmother in the kitchen. "I don't mind. You write that letter, and I'll sign it."

"Don't do me any favors," Grandmother said. "I don't know why I'm being punished so. My daughter marries wrong. My husband is helpless. My grandson sings all day. My life is dust in the air!"

"Stop pitying yourself!" Grandfather told her.

Zheka rolled over on his back.

As he started to drift back into sleep, Grandfather walked into the family room.

"I'm not helpless!" he said bitterly. "I'm a vice-chairman!"

Zheka heard the six separate sounds of a number being dialed.

"Is Comrade Yezhov home?" Grandfather whispered into the mouthpiece. "This is his old friend calling. I'm vice-chairman of the Losinoostrovskaya chapter of the Old Bolsheviks' Union."

He nodded, listening.

"He's *not* home!" Zheka thought.

"I see," Grandfather said. "When did he leave?"

He put the receiver down and stood still a moment.

Zheka held his breath.

Grandfather turned to Zheka and saw that his eyes were open.

"Zheka! My favorite grandson!" he said. "Here you are! Wake up! Let's go to Moscow! I can't wait to get away from that woman!"

"Yes, let's go to Moscow!" Zheka said. He ran into the hallway.

Grandmother silently stepped out of the kitchen.

"We're going to Moscow! It was his idea, not mine!" Zheka told her. "He needs to get away from you!"

"Fine!" she said, and went back into the kitchen.

Grandfather made Zheka put on two pairs of pants and a fur hat.

Zheka and Grandfather headed for the Losinoostrovskaya train station. It was behind a thin tongue of the woods, so close by that late at night the squeals and whistles of the long-distance trains sometimes woke Zheka up.

The two of them trudged down a narrow path that led between the tall pines and firs, past the now empty log cabins, a high school, a barber shop, and a poster plastered to the concrete wall of a new power plant whose slogan, printed in red letters, each the size of Zheka, read: "COMMUNISM = SOVIET POWER + ELECTRIFICATION OF THE ENTIRE COUNTRY!"

They climbed up the slippery, iced-over steps of the train station platform.

"How are you feeling?" Grandfather asked. "Are your teeth still hurting? You seem a little pale. Did you take your medication?"

"I did," Zheka lied, and blushed.

Grandfather nodded and waved at some small, gray-haired man on the opposite side of the platform, across the railway tracks.

"An old bolshevik!" Zheka thought.

When the electric train arrived, Zheka took a corner seat by the window and gazed at the vast expanse of melting snow outside. The sun had disappeared from the sky some time ago, and now everything seemed dreary. The countryside was the cement color of the dull rows of the "Khrushcheville slums," as Zheka's father called them: the concrete-block apartment buildings in the new districts of Moscow and Leningrad.

At some point in the future, Zheka's parents were going to get an apartment there.

In the meantime, Zheka was on his way to Moscow.

Since it was afternoon and everyone had already left for work, the car was half empty. The train sighed and shuddered impatiently.

Grandfather waved his old-bolshevik-and-veteran-of-the-war free monthly pass at the uniformed trainman in a high-peaked cap.

The train pulled out.

The car started rocking from side to side, its cast-iron wheels rattling against the rails. The car door slid open with a screeching sound.

Soon the gray silhouettes of the Moscow skyscrapers—the Ministry of Foreign Affairs, the Hotel Ukraine, the University—rose from the overcast horizon. Grandfather opened his book, *Face to Face with America*. Zheka leaned back and closed his eyes. His headache flared up again. Zheka was afraid he might faint.

He waited. Eventually the pain dissolved into nausea.

At one of the short snowbound stops along the way, an old beggar entered the car. He was haggard-looking, bareheaded, toothless, with a worn-out hat in one hand and a stack of books the size of playing cards in the other.

"Comrades! You're looking at a broken man!" he announced.

No one except Zheka paid him any attention.

He walked unsteadily down the aisle, pausing briefly to stare into the passengers' eyes, waiting in silence for a nod and a handout.

Very few people gave him any money.

The beggar drew level with the bench where Zheka and Grandfather were sitting and held his hat out to them. Its bottom was glistening with small coins.

"Would you care to buy a patriotic calendar for just fifteen kopecks? Your son would love it!" he said in a raspy voice.

Grandfather shook his head no and turned away.

The beggar fixed his blurry eyes on Zheka's face.

"What do you think?" he said.

Zheka looked at the black-and-white pictures in his hands, twelve in all for the number of months in a year. They were photographs of Stalin, former leader of his country who, according to the "Our Leaders" section of Zheka's textbook, was forced into making some serious mistakes toward the end of his life.

His body had recently been moved out of the Tomb in Red Square.

Zheka's father's eyes burned with hatred when he heard Stalin's name.

On the other hand, Zheka's kindergarten teacher had always told them that Stalin was a good and noble man.

It was Stalin's cohorts who gave orders to execute millions of people.

But then, those executed were the *enemies* of the people!

"Stalin!" Zheka liked the sound of that word. It meant "Man of Steel."

Zheka couldn't take his eyes off the pictures.

He, too, wanted to have his face on a calendar!

Zheka glanced around and saw that everyone in the car was now looking at him.

"This kid knows Stalin!" the beggar said, clutching the handrail overhead. He leaned down and patted Zheka's shoulder.

Grandfather pulled the calendar from Zheka's hand.

"Do you want it?" he asked, in doubt. "He's not in fashion these days, you know, but he was a good man!"

Zheka nodded. He imagined how he would bring the calendar home and tack it onto the wall above his bed.

"Who is it?" his friends would ask him.

"Don't you know?" He would raise his eyebrows in surprise. "This is Stalin!"

Grandfather slid a fifteen-kopeck coin from his wallet and dropped it into the beggar's hat.

"Put this thing in your pocket!" he whispered into Zheka's ear.

Zheka tucked the calendar into the pocket of his pants.

"We're both old soldiers, you and me, I can tell!" the beggar said to Grandfather. Swaying from side to side, he walked over to the car door, turned to face the silent passengers and sang in a nasal voice:

I liberated Kiev, I liberated Tallinn.
Look at me now, citizens—where is my health?

I spilled my blood for dear comrade Stalin!
My mother's crying her eyes out in her grave!

He opened the door and disappeared.

The train slowed down with a hissing and sighing of brakes.

Zheka and Grandfather stepped onto the platform of the Yaroslavsky train station.

The cold Moscow air was full of particles of soot.

It took Zheka and Grandfather a while to get used to the sudden jolt of noise all around them.

They joined the faceless, rumbling human flow that carried them all the way to Red Square.

Zheka and Grandfather stood, hand in hand, waiting, at the end of the long line that snaked across Red Square to the Tomb. It was a black-and-red marble box with *Him* inside.

He was the Architect of the Great October Revolution and the Creator of the New World. They called *Him He* in the "He" section of Zheka's textbook. The city where Zheka was born was named after *Him*.

He was the kindest man who ever lived.

Strangely, Zheka's first thought in Red Square was unpleasant. The only person he knew who had dared to speak of *Him* without love was Zheka's own father.

Zheka remembered the incident quite well, even though he had been trying hard to purge it from his memory. That was a long time ago. His younger brother hadn't yet been born. Grandmother was at home in Losinoostrovskaya, but Grandfather was in Leningrad, briefly visiting Zheka's mother.

They were sitting around the dinner table in their room

one night, the four of them, eating and watching the evening news on the new TV. Grandfather and Zheka's father usually never got along, but on that particular occasion they seemed united by the blurry black-and-white images of Red Square.

An endless line to the Tomb appeared on the screen.

Zheka's father chuckled and said: "Good God! Why don't they bury him already? This is ridiculous! The whole world must be laughing at us!"

Grandfather's face turned red. He struck the table with his palm and grimaced with pain.

"Oh, come on! Don't make a scene!" Zheka's father said.

Grandfather got up and walked out the door.

Zheka's mother ran after him into the corridor: "Papa! Papa! Don't take him seriously! That's just the way he is! He didn't mean to offend you! He was only joking!"

Zheka could hear their hushed voices behind the closed door.

"Do it for me! Please!" his mother said.

Grandfather came back to the room and sat rigidly at the table.

That was the end of it.

Zheka hated himself long afterward for not having immediately reported his father's words about *Him* to his kindergarten teacher.

What if his father was an enemy of the people?

This thought made Zheka moan with despair.

He didn't want to think of his father now.

Zheka shook his head and looked around. He had been in Moscow once before, when he was auditioning for the First Moscow Boys Choir, but never in Red Square. Grandfather had always said, when Zheka begged to see the Tomb, that he was too young. What was so unusual about today, then? Zheka didn't know.

He was overtaken by the lightheadedness of unbridled ardor!

The only thing that distracted him from watching the Honor Guards goose-step across the Square toward the Tomb was the steadily growing, throbbing pain in his right ear.

He pulled his hat over his ears and decided to wait it out.

The pain lessened somewhat.

The clock on the Spasskaya Tower, the Kremlin Courants, struck the hour. The guards, two young men no more than eighteen years old, marched solemnly across the square. They stood watch, unblinking, against the front wall of the Tomb. Each one appeared less a human being than an extension of his fixed bayonet. Their faces were blank, their wide-open eyes sheer pewter. The line to the Tomb moved forward in fits and starts. Every quarter of an hour the Tomb bit off and swallowed up a hundred or so awestruck people at a time.

Zheka had never seen so many people before.

He stood there, in the center of the world, within an arm's length of the ancient Kremlin Wall, glimpsing the gilded top of Ivan the Terrible's belltower next to the Beheader's Stump, a historic place of execution on the forbidden side of the Wall.

Zheka suddenly realized that he was the only six year old he knew who was about to enter the Tomb.

His excitement gave way to feverish agitation.

He told himself to calm down.

On his right was GUM, the largest department store in the country. St. Basil's cathedral with its ice-cream swirls of multicolored domes stood straight ahead.

According to Zheka's textbook, the anonymous architect who had built St. Basil's consequently had his eyes gouged out so that he'd never reproduce it anyplace else.

The dark gray Minin and Pozharsky monument was only a few steps away.

There was nothing red about Red Square. According to the "Heart of Your Country" section of Zheka's textbook, "red" in old Russian simply meant "beautiful."

The Kremlin Wall was the color of coagulated blood. Its tooth-edged outline served a quiet warning to an enemy.

It was a symbol of Zheka's country's might.

The Wall was also a cemetery. It contained the cremated remains of the dead leaders of the Party.

Stalin, however, was *not* inside the Wall. No one knew where he was.

Zheka stamped his feet against the cold. He looked up and saw a lonely red balloon soaring high in the sky. He followed it with his eyes, until it coalesced with the clouds.

They were drawing nearer to the Tomb.

Zheka was afraid that people all around him, whispering incessantly in reverent voices, might overhear the beating sound of his heart.

He took off his flap-eared hat and quickly slicked back his hair.

He wished that there had been a mirror hanging from the sky above the Square where he could see if he looked his best.

Zheka knew that he had behaved well ever since they left Losinoostrovskaya.

He glanced up at Grandfather.

"Do you like me?" he asked.

But Grandfather didn't seem to be concerned. He was gazing instead at the back of a man his own age dressed in a military overcoat with sky blue four-star colonel's shoulder straps and a tall Astrakhan hat. He was standing in the line a few meters ahead of them, holding a boy a little older than Zheka by the hand.

The colonel looked over his shoulder, nonplussed, his face rough and rugged, meat-red.

He saw Grandfather and nodded, stretching his lips into the beginnings of a smile. Grandfather half-raised his hand in a greeting. The colonel's boy stuck out his tongue at Zheka.

The Tomb doors solemnly and noiselessly opened. Zheka and Grandfather moved along with the others in line, passing from the gray light of day into the artificial brightness of the Tomb.

They found themselves in a small room.

There, standing to either side of a long table, two men in black, their faces flour-white, prepared the new arrivals for entering the main chambers. Their eyes were red and tired, but watchful. Speaking in a barely audible voice, one of them told Zheka and Grandfather to put their belongings onto the table and raise their arms over their heads. When they had done this, the two men stepped forward and bodysearched everyone in the room.

"Is this your son?" asked one of the two Tomb men, lowering himself on his knees before Zheka. "How old is he? Does he understand where he is? This place is no kindergarten, you know."

He mocked a frightening face to let Zheka know this was nothing serious and he shouldn't be afraid.

"This is my grandson," Grandfather said. He stood with both arms raised, looking like a surrendering German during the War. "His name is Zheka. He's from Leningrad. He's thinking of staying here, with us."

Zheka stared at him. "I'm *not!*" he said.

The man rolled up his eyes and touched Zheka's shoulder. "Hands up!" he ordered.

Zheka threw his hands up.

The man, indifferent and brisk, like a doctor at the hospital, lightly frisked Zheka's body several times.

"What's that in your pocket?" he asked in a sharp suspicious voice.

"A calendar," Zheka breathed out. "Grandfather bought it for me."

"I see," the man said. He reached into Zheka's pants pocket and pulled out the calendar. Scrunching up his nose in disgust, he flipped through the dog-eared little pages with his index finger.

"Are you out of your mind?" he said to Grandfather. "Are you a Stalin lover? What kind of a political statement are you trying to make? Do you want to screw your boy up for good? Do you want to get thrown out of here?"

Grandfather looked miserable. The man tossed the calendar onto the table which by now was cluttered with bags and briefcases, pocketbooks, old cameras, backpacks full of canned lunch meat and sausage.

Everyone looked at Zheka and Grandfather.

"It's just because I'm in a good mood today that I'm letting you in," the man said.

Invisible doors opened in the wall across the room from them. Unspeakably sad music poured in. Everyone lined up two abreast. Grandfather squeezed Zheka's palm in his hand and whispered in his ear: "Now!"

Zheka gulped and nodded.

They entered a large, dim hall and circled the glass sarcophagus where *He* lay with *His* eyes closed on a black velvet bench in *His* tight black woolen suit and black shiny wingtips.

Zheka, half-blinded by the rush of blood to his head, recognized *Him* immediately.

"*He!* The best man who ever lived!" said a deep voice, verging on a sob, coming from beneath a high ceiling. "*He's* still alive! *He's* more alive than any living man! We are all going to die some day, but *He* will live forever!"

Someone whispered: "It's *Him!*"

Zheka took a deep breath and intently peered into *His* wax-yellow face, too ordinary and regular to be *His*, and yet at the same time so familiar that it no longer belonged to *Him* any more than it did to Zheka or anyone else.

What he saw amazed him.

He had no eyes! *His* sockets were empty, hollow beneath dry layers of wrinkled skin! The man Zheka was looking at was *not* more alive than any living man!

He was undeniably dead.

Zheka didn't know what to think. He looked up at Grandfather and saw that his eyes were glistening.

"What's wrong with *him?*" Zheka thought.

He turned away and took a step forward from the line, toward the glass box. Grandfather's hand pulled him back: "Don't ever do that again!"

Zheka shrugged.

He looked and looked, and then, finally, it dawned on him: the man behind the glass was a fake; *His* double, *His* look-alike!

Zheka searched the hall with his eyes to see if someone else had made the same realization, but at that moment the lights went off. The music, a mournful version of "Appassionata" by Ludwig van Beethoven, *His* favorite composition, stopped coming out of the loudspeakers embedded in the walls of the hall.

Their thirty seconds were up. They filed out of the Tomb.

Back in Red Square, nothing seemed to have changed around them. People in line to the Tomb looked at them with envy.

Zheka's head was bursting with pain.

"Let's go!" Grandfather said. He took Zheka's hand and they walked over to where the colonel, Grandfather's acquaintance, stood with his boy by his side, striking a match to light the cigarette in his mouth. As they approached, he cupped the feeble flame in his palms against the wind and said: "We're not getting any younger, are we?"

"No, we're not!" Grandfather said.

He and the colonel embraced.

The colonel's boy spat through the crack between his front teeth and put his hand out for Zheka to shake. Zheka hid his hands behind his back.

"I don't know you!" he said.

The colonel patted Grandfather's shoulder and said: "That's enough. Don't hug me so hard."

Grandfather took a step back from him and turned to Zheka.

"Can you believe this?" he said in an unnatural voice. "Life never ceases to amaze me! Look who we've run into: this is my old friend, Comrade Yezhov! We fought the Germans together!"

The colonel smiled. Zheka inclined his head.

"Yezhov? What a strange coincidence!" he thought.

Wasn't it the name of the man Grandfather was calling from Losinoostrovskaya?

Zheka realized that his grandfather was a liar.

"That's true. We liberated Europe together," the colonel said. "We used to be best friends. But unfortunately, not anymore."

"No, not anymore. I wish we still were, but we are no longer equals." Grandfather sighed. "You're much more important than I am! Come to think of it: chairman of a district chapter of the Old Bolsheviks' Union in Moscow! If I hadn't walked up to you a minute ago, you probably wouldn't have even wanted to talk to me!"

The colonel's boy laughed.

"That's not true!" the colonel objected, winking at Zheka.

Zheka could see, even through the dull film of sickness, that he was almost purring with pleasure, puffing himself up with self-importance.

"Oh, if only I, too, could be made chairman of a district chapter in Moscow, like you—not quite like you, because you are better than the rest of us, but almost like you—I would be of so much greater use to the Party!" Grandfather exclaimed.

He gave the colonel a sly look.

"Have you spoken with Kondrashov?" the colonel asked. "He's currently in charge of these matters. He might be able to help you. You have a telephone at home, why don't you give him a call?"

"But I don't know his number, and he doesn't know *me*," Grandfather admitted. "Besides, I'm not sure he'd even want to talk to me!"

"Let me talk to him about you," the colonel suggested. "I think he'll listen to me."

He and Grandfather stepped aside and continued their conversation with their backs to Zheka and the other boy.

"So!" the boy said, yawning. "You're this clown's grandson? It figures. What's your name?"

Zheka stared at him.

"Are you dumb? What's your name?" the boy repeated.

"Zheka!" Grandfather said loudly. "Why don't you tell your new friend your name?"

The boy laughed again. "Zheka! Like that monkey on TV: Zhakonya! It suits you well! And where do you live?" He touched Zheka's shoulder and quickly drew back his hand.

He was probably no stronger than Zheka.

"Don't touch me anymore," Zheka told him.

The boy gave Zheka a slight shove. "Didn't you hear me?" he said. "I asked you a simple question: where do you live? No, don't answer, let me guess: you live in Khrushcheville, like a rat!"

As Zheka stepped back, surprised that he knew his father's jokes, the boy faked a punch to his stomach.

"Like a rat!" he repeated.

Zheka turned away and said: "I'm from Leningrad. It's the most beautiful city in the world! If I told you about it, you'd die with envy! I don't like Moscow! I'm only here because I've been chosen to sing with the First Moscow Boys Choir!"

The boy puffed his cheeks and then slapped them with his hands.

Zheka tugged at Grandfather's sleeve.

"Just one more minute," Grandfather said. "Can't you see I'm busy?"

Zheka shrugged and looked around him. The square was still crowded with people, but the line to the Tomb was now shorter than it had been before. The March daylight was beginning to darken. He inhaled the damp air. The smell of spring in the wind coming from the Moscow River, the cucumber smell of fresh fish being sold by the kilo from large wooden boxes on every street corner made him think of Leningrad.

"What is it? You don't want to talk to me?" the boy said behind his back. "You're tired of my face? Well, let me tell you something: your grandfather is an idiot, your parents are morons, you're an ugly little monkey, and you can go back to Leningrad, because we don't need you here! There're already too many people in Moscow!"

Zheka only smiled.

"If you were in my kindergarten, you'd always end up being America!" he said.

The boy looked at Zheka's broad smile and burst out laughing.

Grandfather and the colonel turned their heads to see what was going on.

Pleased that their grandsons had found a common language so quickly, they resumed their conversation.

"What's so funny?" Zheka asked, covering his mouth with his hand.

"Your mouth!" the boy said, still laughing. "Have you looked at yourself in the mirror lately? Where are your teeth? They're *gone!* And you went inside the Tomb looking like *that?*" He doubled over, weak with affected merriment.

"Tsh-sh!" the colonel said.

The boy grabbed Zheka's hand, lifted it up to his mouth and playfully bit Zheka's index finger.

"You pig!" Zheka screamed.

He swung his arm and struck the boy across the mouth with his open palm. The boy fell on his back and let out a thin squeal.

The tail end of the line to the Tomb stirred uneasily.

"Shut up!" Zheka kicked the boy with his foot.

The boy stared at him in horror.

"Do you want more? Get up and fight!" Zheka said. He clenched his teeth.

Zheka imagined himself, a good man, ruthless when needed, kind when necessary. He liked himself at this moment.

Zheka felt sick.

He shouldn't have clenched his teeth. Now he was in great pain again. A swollen gland at the side of his right jaw threatened to make him vomit.

The boy sat up on the cobblestones of Red Square.

Grandfather squeezed Zheka's shoulders and gave him a jolt.

"Are you out of your mind?" he hissed. "What's wrong with you? Have you lost your mind?"

Zheka realized that his punishment was going to be worse than anything he had ever been through in his life. "But he deserved it!" he whispered.

The colonel stepped in. "Don't punish him! You should

be proud of him!" he said. "Your little Zheka's a brave boy!
It was all my grandson's fault!"

"That's right!" Zheka said.

Grandfather, however, wouldn't leave Zheka alone. "You
must apologize!" he said. His face was pale.

Zheka saw with dismay that his grandfather was scared.

"Say that you're sorry, or I'll be ashamed of you!"
Grandfather said, shaking Zheka's shoulders. "Do it for me!
You should be ashamed of yourself! That's how you love
Him: you start a fight in front of the Tomb!"

He pushed Zheka toward the boy who was rubbing his
dry eyes with the back of his hand.

Zheka blinked, forcing back the angry tears.

"But you don't really love *Him!*" he told Grandfather.
"You're just saying it—that you love *Him!* But the truth is,
you don't really care about *Him*, none of you! You're all
liars!"

Weak, embarrassing tears finally began to stream down
his cheeks.

"Now-now-now," the colonel said. "What is going on
here? People might think we're torturing the kid!"

"He's a psycopath, I told you!" said the colonel's boy.

"He's tired and sick," Grandfather said. "He doesn't
know what he's talking about."

He hugged Zheka.

Zheka pushed him off.

"*Him!* I'm talking about *Him!*" he cried out. "Remember when we were all sitting in our room in Leningrad,
watching Red Square and the Tomb on TV? You were there
too! Dad laughed and said that they should've buried *Him*
a long time ago. You asked him what the hell kind of talk
was that, and you left! But later you came back to the table,
as if nothing happened, and said nothing, and did nothing!
You let him get away with it! Remember? If you don't, I
do!"

He knew that he shouldn't have spoken.

"Shut up!" Grandfather slapped his face with his open palm and pushed him away. Zheka almost fell down.

He glowered at Grandfather and ran over to the colonel. "Let me be *your* grandson!" he said.

The colonel pushed him gently away. "Do something! This is embarrassing!" he told Grandfather.

The colonel's boy laughed again.

"I'm sorry, I'm sorry!" Grandfather said. "I love you, Zheka! You're my grandson! It's just that you're telling lies! Where did you get that awful story from? Tell us you've dreamed it! Please!"

He stroked Zheka's head.

"I didn't dream it!" Zheka said.

"I think he's already said more than enough," the colonel said. "I find what he just told us very interesting. Maybe we should bury *Him*, huh?" He slid another cigarette from the pack inside his overcoat pocket and struck the match on the matchbox.

"But that's not how it actually happened!" Grandfather exclaimed. "That's his inflamed imagination! He's just a kid! He's got a toothache! He must have taken too much medication this morning! I can explain: when I last visited my daughter, we had a serious conversation. I told her that she should leave her husband! I'm writing a letter to his Party Committee about his behavior! I would have never sat at the same table with a man of opposing views!"

"But it seems like you already had," the colonel pointed out. "Frankly, I'm disappointed in you."

His face was sad, hard. He took his smiling grandson's hand. They walked slowly away.

Grandfather just stood there, his head bowed.

"America!" Zheka thought, suddenly dead tired, unable to catch his breath.

"What's wrong with me?" he thought.

He should have told Grandfather when they were still in Losinoostrovskaya that he hadn't taken his medication in the morning.

Zheka sat down on the mud-covered cobblestones. He felt sleepy. "I lied to you today!" he confessed.

"You can say that again!" Grandfather shook his fist. "Do you know how we used to treat a traitor during the War? Just wait till we get home!"

He picked Zheka up and carried him out into one of the broad streets that flowed into the Square. In no time they were at the Yaroslavsky train station.

When they got off the train in Losinoostrovskaya, it was already dark. The air was crisp and cold. Zheka thought, "Soon we'll be able to see the White Nights!" Then he remembered where he was: *not* in Leningrad.

Moscow was too far south for the long summer days.

Soon Zheka was alone in his room. He lay on his back and stared at the ceiling. Grandmother made him gulp down two white pills with a large cup of hot milk and tucked a thermometer underneath his arm.

It turned out that he had a temperature.

At night, still half awake, he listened to his grandparents' indistinct conversation in the family room and the low voice of Yuri Levitan on the kitchen radio. It was the second time in one day that Zheka heard that voice.

"Their memory will live in our hearts forever!" Yuri Levitan intoned.

"Turn that thing off, for crying out loud!" Grandfather said.

Grandmother got up from the couch and went into the kitchen.

The radio fell silent.

Zheka guessed by the muting of the howling wind outside that it had begun to snow again.

Grandmother spoke in the family room.

"You should have reminded me to give him his medicine before you two left. It's all your fault!" she said.

There was a pause.

"Don't blame *me*. I don't even want to talk about that little traitor!" Grandfather said. He got up from the couch. "I've got plenty to worry about. Who knows what they're going to do to me? One thing is certain: I'm not a vice-chairman anymore!"

His soft slippers shuffled on the floor.

"Now-now-now," Grandmother said.

Zheka thought: "Does this mean they'll take away our telephone?"

"I'm getting old!" Grandfather said.

Zheka yawned.

Gray spots of light were slowly shifting across the stucco ceiling.

"Now-now-now. Calm down. It'll be all right," Grandmother said. "Don't panic. After all, who's going to pay attention to a six year old?"

"Colonel Yezhov already did," Grandfather said. "You should've seen his face!"

He resumed his pacing around the room.

Zheka could no longer stay awake.

He rubbed his eyes.

The telephone rang.

Grandfather picked it up.

"Yes. I'm listening," he whispered. Zheka felt warm. His head was heavy.

"No, my grandson didn't dream them up!" Grandfather said. "They were regular gypsies! My grandson saw them! He's a very bright little boy! He never lies!"

"The gypsies!" Zheka thought.

Grandfather's steps approached Zheka's door.

Zheka opened his eyes and shivered with fear.

"Do you think he's asleep?" Grandfather asked.

"Don't bother him! He's got a cold!" Grandmother said.

Grandfather went back to the couch.

The telephone rang again. This time Grandmother picked it up.

"Are you out of your mind? Do you know what time it is?" she said angrily.

The next moment her tone of voice changed to that of love mixed with surprise.

"It's you!" she cried out. "My love! Where are you calling from? The post office? Are they still open? It's late!"

Zheka began to fall asleep.

He awoke with a start. Grandmother was talking with his mother in the family room.

"Oh my poor girl!" she crooned. "Don't worry, he'll be back! You'll see! And if he isn't, forget about him! Just imagine he's dead!"

Grandmother sobbed.

"Oh, please!" Grandfather moaned.

Zheka sat up in his bed.

"I wish I were with you now!" Grandmother said. "Then I could hug you! We'd cry together! Please, don't tell me you want to die! You're breaking my heart!"

"Tell her: if somebody's going to die in this family, it's not going to be her!" Grandfather grumbled.

"Not me either!" Zheka thought. He imagined Grandfather and Grandmother out in the family room.

They were both old.

She was sitting on a worn-out couch, knitting.

He was standing beside her with his hand on her shoulder.

Their features were serene in the soft glow of the yellow lightbulb inside the pink lampshade overhead.

That was how Zheka was going to remember Grand-mother and Grandfather: as a picture in the "Your Family" section of his textbook.

The lights in the house went off. Zheka fell asleep. In his dream he saw a ghastly city.

It was a city with poisoned blood. Zheka recognized it. He had lived there, too.

Gray shadows fell on the roofs of run-down tenements; a siren went off inside a gloomy factory. Sullen crowds of men and women filled the narrow streets. They were headed to the Factory Wall.

It was strange to think that all of them had long since been dead.

Soon the sun rolled out onto the sky. It woke him up.

Zheka peered intently through the plum-colored dark of his room. He couldn't tell whether someone was sitting in a chair next to his bed.

Zheka hoisted himself up on his elbow.

His tongue scraped against something sharp at the back of his jaw. There was a subtle taste of blood in his mouth.

The wind outside had died down. From off in the dis-tance, stray dogs howled at the sickle of the moon. A long-distance train, Moscow–Leningrad, roared by and sped across the night.

A strange smell was in his room, like musty mothballs and shoeshine.

Zheka's heart filled with joy and love.

"The Archangel Gabriel!" he thought. "He's here!"

Old Seraphima would have crossed herself and made a wish. Zheka made a wish.

He reached out with his hand and touched the naked skin of a man's wrist.

"Zheka? Is that you?" asked an unmistakable voice. Strong fingers gently squeezed his palm.

"Yes," Zheka whispered.

"Wake up!" the voice said.

Zheka waited.

After a while a face broke through the lessening dark. Zheka made out the pointed beard, the huge forehead.

"So, Zheka!" *He* said, leaning forward. "I'm told you love me very much! I love you too. What do you want from me?"

Zheka lay back down.

"You know what I want!" he said.

"But what can you do?" *He* asked. "Can you sing?"

Zheka opened his mouth and sang:

The tree blossoms were thick in the air
Beyond the Factory Walls. Hungry, cold . . .

"This song is so wonderful!" he thought.

"No-no! I don't like that song!" *He* said. "Sing something else!"

Zheka started singing the beginning of "Moscow Nights." It had nothing to do with the Revolution.

Van Cliburn, the curly-haired winner of the Tchaikovsky Competition, played it on TV two years ago.

He was an American, the only one who could sing in Zheka's language.

Even the Americans admitted it was one of the best songs in the world!

Zheka imagined a green garden awash in moonlight.

Not a sound, not a rustle. Summer. August.

In Leningrad, Zheka's mother is asleep. The silver river is quiet.

Zheka's father is not at home. He's at the library. Grandmother wants him dead for some reason.

Old Seraphima is moaning and whispering out in the corridor.

The Kremlin Courants, glowing red, strike the loneli-
est hour of the night. The Honor Guards are *not* asleep.

A drunk man is pounding against the door of a log cabin
on the other side of the street. "Open up! I'm freezing out
here!" he shouts. His wife, fed up with his antics, refuses to
let him in.

Oh, if only you could know
How I cherish those
Dear Mo-o-oscow nights!

Zheka opened his eyes and saw that now they were
singing together. *He* hugged Zheka and kissed him on the
forehead. Zheka squinted at *Him*, trying to see if *He* had
eyes.

He couldn't make them out in the deep shadow on *His*
face.

Their voices rose to the ceiling and all the way up to
the sky. Zheka tilted his head back farther.

Never before had he sung quite so beautifully.

If somebody could hear him now, he would instantly
be accepted by the First Moscow Boys Choir.

If their communal apartment neighbors could see him
now, they would never have let him leave for Moscow!

Zheka cut himself short. The pain in his mouth grew
stronger.

"How about my wish?" he said. "Haven't I been good?"

"What wish? After what you've done to Seraphima?"
He said.

A soft hand firmly pressed against Zheka's chest. *He*
got up from *His* chair.

"I thought you were singing simply because you love
me, but now I can see I was wrong!" *He* said. "I'm disappointed in you! Now it's time for me to go back to the Tomb!"

He stepped back from Zheka's bed and disappeared into the air.

"How strange!" Zheka thought. "If *He* needs to be back in the Tomb, that means he's dead!"

The thought was so upsetting that Zheka couldn't keep from crying. He screamed.

His howling woke his grandparents up.

They burst into his room.

Grandmother put her cool hand on his forehead.

"Call emergency. He's very hot! I don't know what's wrong with him!" she said over her shoulder.

Grandfather bolted out the door and was away in the family room for a long time.

When he returned, his face was flushed with indignation. "Busy, busy all the time!" he said. "When you need them, suddenly they're very busy! Nothing works like it should around here!"

"Don't just stand there! *Do* something!" Grandmother said.

Grandfather went to the kitchen and brought Zheka a glass of hot tea and jars of honey and strawberry preserves.

Grandmother went to the family room and, shaking her head, brought Zheka his textbook.

"Here!" she said. "Look: your favorite book! But I'm warning you: it's going to make you feel even worse!"

Grandmother and Grandfather stood solemnly in the dusk by his bedside.

"Take a good look at him—don't you think the right side of his face is swollen?" Grandmother asked.

"I can't see," Grandfather said.

"Turn on the light," Grandmother said.

"No, don't!" Zheka protested.

The light was bright.

Grandmother squeezed his chin with her fingers and looked into his mouth.

"Look!" she cried out triumphantly. "He's cutting new teeth! There, in the wisdom corner!"

"Let me see," Grandfather said.

Zheka sat there with his mouth open.

Grandfather reached far into his mouth with his index finger and touched the beginning of a new tooth.

"Ouch!" he said, frowning in mock pain. "It's sharp! But it's a little early, don't you think? This *can't* be a wisdom tooth! He's only six years old!"

"So what?" Zheka said. Grandmother and Grandfather laughed.

"Close your mouth!" Grandmother told him.

"Congratulations!" Grandfather said. "Now you can call yourself a grown-up!"

Zheka stared at them in disbelief. *Congratulations?*

Didn't they see how inconsolable he was?

He decided that neither Grandfather nor Grandmother knew what was going to happen to them.

Zheka looked into their animated faces to make sure there was no sadness lurking behind their odd cheeriness.

They were smiling!

"What's wrong with them?" he thought.

"Now what?" Grandmother asked. "Now that everything has been explained, what are you crying for?"

"You're going to die!" Zheka said.

Kiss

It's morning again. Zheka, Tolyan, and Yulka are in
Zheka's room. Zheka's parents are at work now, and
his younger brother Dima is in a day nursery across the
street, but they, too, live in this room, and when they come
back home in the evening, the room will no longer be Zheka's
only.

Particles of dust whirl slowly in the cone of light cutting through the pale and placid air. The room is not large.
There are dust-jacketed books on the shelves, a bed, a table,
a mirror, some pictures on the walls, some chairs at the
table, two reclining armchairs—for Zheka and his younger
brother to sleep on—a KVN TV set, and a ladybug, God's
little cow, crawling along the windowsill: it shines and
sparkles in the sun in the open window. Tolyan runs to the
window and squashes the ladybug with his fist. "Zheka-
Zheka-Zheka!" he says.

Zheka shakes his head.

"Zheka-Zheka-Zheka!" Tolyan repeats lazily.

Yulka steps over to the table with her hands behind her back. Now she can see Tolyan's face better. She can see herself in the mirror better now, too. She squints her eyes. "Tolyan! Let's play!" She smiles and squints.

"Shut up, Yulka!" Tolyan says, squatting on his heels, then falling down on the floor. "Zheka-Zheka, be a real man!" Zheka shakes his head.

"You're a wimp!" Tolyan says, laughing. Zheka shakes his head.

Yulka makes a scary face at herself in the mirror and giggles. Zheka takes a step toward the bookshelves, looking at Yulka. Yulka runs to the window. Tolyan jumps over Zheka's favorite chair, kicks it, then straightens up. They stand still for a second.

Zheka pushes another chair with his leg. "My mother doesn't want us to play cards, Tolyan."

Tolyan only snorts. Yulka giggles.

"Your mother doesn't want you to play with me either," Tolyan says, jumping into Dima's armchair. Yulka giggles again. She's not articulate. Zheka climbs into his own chair. Tolyan sits up, falls face down on the floor, crawls over to the window. "Do you know where she hides the deck?" he asks.

Zheka shakes his head.

"I didn't think so," Tolyan says, sounding disappointed.

Yulka giggles, still making faces at herself in the mirror. Tolyan pulls himself up onto the windowsill, looks down, where the breeze is sunny. The air vibrates over the back yard. "Come here, Zheka-Zheka!" Tolyan says.

Zheka extricates himself from the warm dough of the armchair's innards and stands in the middle of the room. "Hey, Tolyan!" he says. "Do you know the word 'extricate'? I just thought: you're strong, but do you know many words?" He cuts a glance at Yulka. She pays no attention.

"Grow up and be a man," Tolyan says, looking intently at something down below.

Yulka runs to the window. "Let's play doctor!" she says, shyly lowering her eyelashes and then throwing them open dramatically, widening her eyes, looking at Tolyan's back as he rests his stomach cautiously on the windowsill and lets his legs hang loose some fifty centimeters from the floor.

"Yulka, shut your trap! Zheka, you wimp, come here!" Tolyan says, looking down at something at the bottom of the airshaft.

The air is warm, the month is August, the year is 1961, the place is downtown Leningrad, near Varshavsky train station, and none of this matters to any of the three.

Tolyan is the oldest: he is seven and starts school in September. But he's not likely to do well. His strength is in his biceps. He's bulging with muscles, like the weightlifter Yury Vlasov, the Olympic champion. Zheka is aware that Tolyan is bad news altogether—both of his parents are alcoholics, and his father did time in jail, as did many of his father's friends, set free by Uncle Nikita's amnesty in the year that Tolyan was born. Unlike them, Yulka's parents are intelligent. They are intelligentsia, engineers, the cream of the crop. Yulka is attractive. She is six. Zheka, too, is six, and his parents are also intelligentsia. Their families all live in the same apartment, with several other families and a single old woman, Faina. There are eight or more rooms in the apartment; it's huge. Always submerged in semi-dark, it smells of fried cabbage and chlorine.

"Take a look, Zheka-Zheka," Tolyan says, looking out the window. "This is interesting. See that clown sitting on the bench?"

"Clown!" Yulka exclaims, rushing to the window. Tolyan pushes her aside.

"What?" Zheka is hesitant. A clown? Tolyan's words sometimes mean something they don't say.

"A man," Tolyan says patiently, without so much as a look at the two of them, and then permits a glistening string of saliva from his mouth to grow into a heavy drop, shuddering and swaying in the breeze, perfect and complete, only to be sucked back in with a whistle. Then the saliva teasingly starts to grow again . . . and then Tolyan spits, aiming at the head of the man reading a newspaper on the bench below. He misses. The man never looks up. "A man, Zheka," Tolyan says. "Ever heard that word? You know only all those fancy words that do you no good. You should really learn some serious words."

"Let's play doctor, Tolyan!" Yulka sings, waltzing slowly around the room with her eyes on Tolyan's arched back.

"Get lost, Yulka," Tolyan says. "I'm not in the mood for silliness."

Playing doctor means, simply, touching and kissing each other. Yulka loves playing doctor with Tolyan. Of course, her parents wouldn't approve, but who asks them? Zheka would like to kiss Yulka, but Yulka wouldn't allow it. She'd prefer Tolyan, who's older and more manly, although he doesn't seem to care too much for kissing Yulka: Tolyan thinks Yulka isn't bright enough. As far as Zheka is concerned, Tolyan isn't too bright either. Tolyan knows, however, that Zheka is intelligent and quick: unlike Tolyan and Yulka, he can read and write.

Tolyan and Zheka look at the man on the bench, six stories down. Then Tolyan gives Zheka a strong shove with his shoulder, slips off the windowsill onto the floor, and runs off. Zheka chases him out, into the long, dark corridor. Yulka follows them, shaking her head to rearrange her hair.

They speed along the corridor, zigzagging, skirting the rows of jars with homemade preserves and pickled mushrooms, ducking under the wheels of old bicycles covered with shreds of prewar newspapers hanging from the painted walls. "Drop dead!" Zheka screams at the top of his lungs.

They turn right, turn left, turn right, and stop momentarily on the border of dim light in the kitchen. Yulka giggles. Old Faina is stooped over the communal gas stove, stirring with a long and heavy wooden spoon something thick that's cooking in her pot. Before Faina fixes her usual fearful and malicious stare upon them, they turn and race back along the corridor, trying to grab and pinch each other from behind.

"He's still there!" Tolyan says, climbing onto the windowsill again. Yulka resumes her waltzing around the room, bumping into the chairs, knocking them down, humming along with the loud music coming from the second-floor window across the back yard: "Bésame, bésame mucho!"— mellow, tender, loving voices in sombreros. The air is clear, warm, and golden. "Let's send the creep a note!" Tolyan says, gazing down at the man on the bench.

Zheka looks at him.

"What's *bessamay*?" Yulka asks, dancing over to the bookshelves, touching a seashell from Sevastopol, Zheka's father's present on his birthday. "Is it 'hug me'? No, wait, I know: it's 'kiss me'! Bessamay, bessamay, bessamay!"

"Don't touch it, you fool!" Zheka shouts, jumping off the table. Yulka runs back to the door and stands there, waiting and smiling, squinting. She thinks Zheka thinks her eyes are beautiful. Tolyan spits on the man's head again. "Shit!" he says, when he sees that he has missed once more.

Zheka touches the shell with his fingertips, then takes it off the shelf carefully, puts it up to his ear: it roars distantly. He sticks his nose inside: its smell is bitter, salty, dry, and strong, and sweet.

Tolyan lazily walks up to the shelf, snatches the shell from Zheka's hands, jabs Zheka in the ribs with his elbow, buries his nose between the shell's hard porcelain halves, then throws it at Zheka. Zheka dodges and the shell hits the door. Tolyan jumps on him and they fall to the floor.

Tolyan locks his arm around Zheka's neck, squeezes hard, and then lets go. "Wimp!" he says. Zheka, his face red, picks up the shell from the floor, puts it up on its place on the shelf. Yulka giggles. Tolyan jumps into Zheka's armchair, wiggles his legs in the air.

"Tolyan, have you changed your mind? Let's write that man a note!" Zheka says, looking at Yulka.

Tolyan sits up. "Good idea! Let's do it!" he says.

"How boring!" says Yulka, running over to the window.

"Yulka, shut up," Tolyan says, looking at Zheka.

Zheka reaches up on tiptoes, grabs a piece of paper from on top of four or five books that crash to the floor. "Yulka, get a pencil!" he orders. Yulka smiles at him scornfully. She hoists her skirt up over her pink panties and bulges out her belly.

"Yulka, go get a pencil," Tolyan says.

Yulka bites her lower lip and rushes out, picks up a pencil from the chair under the telephone hanging on the wall in the corridor, and jumps back into the room: "Here you go, Tolyan."

Tolyan shakes his head and nods at Zheka. Yulka shrugs and turns away. Zheka keeps standing quietly at the bookshelves. Yulka throws the pencil at him: "Catch!" Zheka dodges.

"Come on, Zheka!" Tolyan says, moving to the table. Zheka picks up the pencil from the floor.

"Very well. What do you want to tell him?" he asks, pulling Dima's armchair closer and rocking the chair, which is less comfortable than his, until it tips over and falls to the floor with a bang.

"Let's tell him he's an asshole," Tolyan says, smiling at himself in the mirror.

Yulka screams with laughter. "What's an asshole, Tolyan?" she asks.

"It's you," Tolyan says.

Yulka pouts. She leans against the door and slams it shut with her back. Zheka tilts his head to his shoulder, sticks out the tip of his tongue, and standing on tiptoes, grabs the pencil in his fist like a pirate's dagger in a TV cartoon.

"We are watching you!" he writes slowly. Each line in every letter comes out taller than the pencil in his hand. He steps back, tilts his head to another shoulder, looks at his words. He is pleased.

"Remarkable!" he says. Tolyan jabs him in the back with his fist. Yulka picks up the paper from the table and moves her red lips in silence. Tolyan snatches the paper from her hands. "Does it say he's an asshole?" he asks, studying the letters. He looks up at Zheka over the edge of the sheet.

Zheka nods. Yulka looks at him, then turns away.

"What if he's gone, Tolyan?" Zheka asks. Tolyan runs to the window, looks down, shakes his head.

"Still there . . . asshole," he says, spitting contentedly. "What do you think? Should we maybe make this little love letter into an airplane and kind of glide it down to him?"

"No, Tolyan, look. . . ." It occurs to Zheka that he's got a better idea. He falls down on the floor and rolls over to Yulka's feet. Yulka laughs and steps over him. Then he looks at Tolyan again.

"No, Tolyan, I've got a much better idea. Let's tie the note on a piece of thread and drop it on his head! Do you have any thread?"

"Sure!" says Tolyan. He walks out of the room as Yulka lounges back in a sour slouch against the wall, yawning and singing "bessamay, bessamay. . ." Zheka jumps at her, kicks her in the ass. She springs up, spreading her fingers, aiming at his face and hissing. Tolyan runs back into the

room with a spool of white thread in his hand. He pushes
Yulka aside and hands the spool to Zheka. Zheka begins to
unreel the thread.

Tolyan picks up the piece of paper from the table and
folds it neatly into a plane. Zheka pricks the tail of the plane
with a needle from the spool. Tolyan pushes the thread
through the hole and ties the loop into a tight knot. He
spools off more thread. "Here we go," he says, looking down
at the man on the bench. Zheka holds the plane in his
hand.

Yulka steps behind Zheka and jabs her shoulder into
his back, pushing him out the window. He starts to fall, but
Tolyan catches him by his collar and pulls him back.

The plane in the meantime has dropped from Zheka's
fingers, and now it's spinning in the warm and buoyant air
as Tolyan keeps slowly spooling off more and more thread.
Zheka holds his breath. The plane bobs over the man's head.
Then Tolyan drops the thread, and the plane gently, softly
lands on the man's head. Yulka giggles.

The man looks up in anger. Of course, he can't see them.
Still, they duck and hide beneath the windowsill, rolling
on the floor in silent laughter. Tolyan tries to hike up the
thread, playfully, but it won't go. Tolyan pulls at it hard.
It's as if a giant fish had swallowed the bait. Zheka and
Tolyan peer down. The man, squinting against the sun, looks
at them, smiling.

And then the thread lifts and the plane glides from the
man's lap. Tolyan catches it in midair and runs with it to
the door. Yulka follows him, making little faces at herself
in the mirror. She stands on tiptoe, trying to look over his
shoulder as Tolyan unfolds the plane. He glances at Zheka.
There are new words written on the paper, beneath Zheka's.
Tolyan and Yulka look at them.

"Zheka?" There's a question mark in Tolyan's voice.

Zheka yawns, stretches, takes the paper from Tolyan's hands, and lifts it up to his face. He pays no attention to Yulka.

The man's handwriting, like Zheka's, is tall, but it looks more mature, although Zheka immediately can tell that the man is not too literate: there's a comma missing. Zheka reads the blue and inky words to himself: "Well come down and let's play!" He purses his lips and drops the paper on the table.

"What's it say?" Tolyan asks anxiously.

Zheka shakes his head. "You don't want to know. It's bad, Tolyan."

"What's it say?" Tolyan asks impatiently.

Zheka sighs. "It says, 'I'll break your necks, you sissies.' "

"Oh," says Tolyan.

Yulka chuckles, then looks at Zheka and smiles. Tolyan turns to her and she steps back, into the dark corner of the room. There's a pause. Tolyan seems uncertain.

They stand still for a second. Then the phone rings in the corridor. They rush out of the room, waving their arms.

Old Faina answers the phone. Nobody ever calls her, but she always answers it nonetheless. It probably reminds her that she is still around. Her voice is even older than she looks.

"Yep," she says into the phone. "That's right. She did pass away." She lowers her eyes, full of old anger that is like yellow water in a dead pond a block away from where all of them live, and looks at Zheka. "It's about your dear mom's aunt," she says, and starts to cough. She's a smoker. Even though they know that they shouldn't giggle, they still do. Faina looks away from them in disgust. "I don't know," she says into the phone. "You'll have to call back later, dear woman. Yes, they did go to work today. Why? I don't know.

Maybe because they love their work so much. . . . That's right, more than they love their relatives. . . . You too. . . . You too. . . . You too. . . . Go in peace."

The children hurry back into Zheka's room as Faina hangs up the phone.

Zheka's grandmother's sister, Aunt Aza, died yesterday, and the phone rang all last night.

Tolyan, whistling some tune through the crack between his teeth, spits on the floor, as if nothing had happened, as if there had been no man on the bench in the back yard. He wants to look calm.

"Zheka! What's that about your aunt?" he asks, climbing on the table.

"Aunt Aza!" Zheka says. Yulka bursts out laughing: the name is funny.

"What about her?" Tolyan asks, doing push-ups on the table. Five, ten, fifteen. He wants to be in shape.

"She died," Zheka says, crossing the room. He pulls his brother's armchair closer to the table and looks around. Yulka stares at herself in the mirror.

"Oh. She what?" Tolyan is lying flat on the table, resting after the push-ups. "Kicked the bucket, huh?"

"Died," Zheka says, jumping over two chairs at once and falling on the floor with a thud.

"Oh. That's too bad, I guess," says Tolyan, and he runs to the window: "He's still there! Dirty punk! Let's write him one more time! Zheka, write!"

Zheka, too, walks to the window and sees the man still reading the newspaper. "*Pravda*," he thinks. "Must be a very interesting paper," he says.

Yulka snorts and yawns.

"Zheka, write!" Tolyan repeats, banging his fist into his palm. "Let's show him! What are you waiting for?"

"Okay, Tolyan," Zheka says, smiling. "Don't get so excited. What do you want me to say this time?"

"Tell him: my daddy'll kill you, you dirty chicken!" Tolyan says.

Yulka giggles again. Zheka nods. He unfolds the paper, bends over the inconvenient windowsill, sticks out his tongue, impatiently shaking his head, and begins to write: "We are up here! My name is Zheka. Who are you?" This time, because there's less room on the paper, his letters are uglier and smaller than before.

While he writes, Yulka scuffles her feet on the floor, whining in a thin voice behind his back. "Boring, boring, boring!" she sings. He knows that she knows that he's afraid that she might try to push him out the window again. If that happens, he will be dead. He should keep an eye on her, but then he'd lose his concentration.

"Tolyan," he says. "Watch Yulka!"

Tolyan is angry now. "Yulka," he says slowly, and Yulka steps back, angry, too.

Tolyan folds the paper into a plane—although it's a different plane now—and drops it on the bench. He's all business. No teasing games this time around.

The man looks up, smiling, and unfolds the paper. He reads it, and still smiling, looks up. He gets a pen from his jacket pocket, writes something on the paper, and then waves at them. Tolyan and Zheka don't hide under the windowsill this time. Tolyan pulls up the plane, shivering with excitement, spitting on the floor.

Zheka catches and unfolds the plane. As he reads the paper slowly, moving his lips, as if he couldn't read with his eyes only, Tolyan watches. But of course, he can't read Zheka's lips. Zheka is much smarter than he is. Yulka smiles at Zheka, looks at Tolyan. The note says: "Come down don't be afraid I have some candy for you! I need to ask you something!"

A lot of letters. Many words.

"Zheka! What's it say?" Tolyan tugs at Zheka's sleeve.

"Yes, tell us: what does it say?" Yulka pipes in.

"It says: "I can beat up your dinky daddy a hundred times." Zheka smiles. "I'm really sorry, Tolyan."

"Oh!" Tolyan says, and adds a short word that neither Zheka nor Yulka understands. It sounds rather unpleasant. Yulka's parents don't let her play with Tolyan precisely because he knows those words, and Zheka's mother doesn't like it either when Zheka and Tolyan play together. But everybody is at work. The children are alone.

Tolyan walks over to the table under Zheka's knowing, steely stare and closes his eyes.

"Let's go downstairs together and let that asshole try and touch us with one finger. Then we'll turn him in to the militia," he suggests. "What do you think?"

Yulka hides her eyes from Tolyan. She's not allowed to go downstairs alone without her parents' permission, and neither is Zheka. But who would know? It's just that Zheka doesn't like the idea. He shakes his head quietly: no. No, Tolyan.

"I see," Tolyan says. "Zheka! Let's write him one more time! Just one more time."

Zheka looks at Yulka in indecision, but now Yulka is hiding her eyes from both of them. Of course, she would rather play doctor! Then Zheka makes up his mind. "Sure, Tolyan. What do you want me to write?" he says.

"Tell him," Tolyan says, getting a little pale. "Tell him: get out of here, or very soon you'll be dead!"

Yulka screws up her face, holding back the tears, and runs out of the room. She's scared. Her steps can be heard down the corridor.

"There's not enough room left on the paper, Tolyan," Zheka points out.

"I don't care," Tolyan says. "I mean, I'm asking you. Please."

Zheka shrugs his shoulder. "All right."

"Drop 'very soon' though," Tolyan says. "He'll under-stand."

Zheka nods.

He writes, in the smallest letters yet: "You only have candy? That's all? I'm disappointed." But he's not. As a matter of fact, he's very pleased with himself.

Tolyan intently watches the man down below. He is still reading his newspaper. Tolyan spits and misses again. The man remains motionless.

"I know what he's doing down there," Tolyan says, dropping the plane from his hands.

"What?" Zheka asks, watching the man on the bench look up at them, smile, and wave. He unfolds the paper, reads the message, writes something. Then he folds the plane back and waves his hand again.

"He's playing with fire," Tolyan says, pulling up the thread.

"What? What do you think he's doing down there, Tolyan?" Zheka asks.

"He's a hired killer," Tolyan says simply, pulling up the thread. "I know. My dad's told me lots of times about weasels like him. It's a common thing."

Zheka stares blankly at Tolyan. "You've got to be kidding me," he says.

Tolyan catches the plane and looks at Zheka with hope: "Zheka! Read!"

Zheka strains his vision. The letters are so tiny this time that it's very hard to recognize all of them. After a while, Zheka realizes that he just can't put them together. He smiles. Then, looking up at Tolyan, he frowns and shakes his head.

"Why were you smiling?" Tolyan asks suspiciously.

"Because he doesn't understand that he's playing with fire," Zheka explains.

"Go ahead, read," Tolyan says. "Please. You don't want me to hit you, do you?"

Zheka reads: " 'Your dad is strong but dumb. I'm smart. There's nothing he can do. Get lost forever.' I'm very sorry, Tolyan."

"Are you sure that's what it says?" Tolyan asks after a pause.

Before Zheka can nod yes, the doorbell rings. Zheka and Yulka rush to the door. Faina shuffles along the corridor quickly. No one ever comes to visit her. She pushes Zheka and Yulka aside. "Who's there?" she asks in her screechy voice.

"It's me!" a woman says from behind the door. "It's Zheka's mother's sister, Aunt Bella!"

"She doesn't know yet!" Zheka whispers to Yulka. She looks at him and winks. While Faina fumbles at the door, they hide behind her back.

Where Aunt Bella lives, in a new district of Leningrad, she doesn't have a telephone. She usually drops in for a visit once or twice a week. She doesn't have children. She's not good-looking. She isn't even married.

Faina unlatches the door, at last, and Aunt Bella steps in. Zheka and Yulka jump at her. "She's dead! She's dead!" they scream. "She's dead as a doornail!"

"Aunt Bella, Auntie Aza's dead!" Zheka shouts triumphantly. Aunt Bella falls back. She drops her two tote bags, full of potatoes, on the dark floor. Zheka and Yulka race back to Zheka's room. It's quiet, peaceful. Tolyan is gone. Zheka runs to the window. The man is still sitting on the bench in the back yard.

"You're an asshole," Yulka says to Zheka, slamming the door shut with her back.

"Oh yeah?" Zheka is taken aback. "Why? What makes you think so?"

"You know why," she says, looking away. "You think you're the only one who can read?"

"Oh, don't be silly," Zheka says in his adult voice. "Look, Yulka, you're a pretty girl and all that, but let's face it, you're not a reader!" He looks again at the new message the man below has written. Now he seems to be able to read almost all of it: "Come on down! Come on! Those who don't take chances don't get to drink the champagne!" And there's something else scribbled on the paper beneath the last line. But what?

Yulka studies Zheka's face. "Do you really think I'm pretty?" she asks in a small voice. He charges into her, hitting her hard in the stomach with his head. Yulka flees from the room. It's getting dark.

Other voices are heard in the corridor. People are coming home. The day will soon be over. Yulka's parents are back; they talk almost inaudibly in their room. Tolyan's mother drags her feet along the corridor, muttering the ugly words Tolyan has learned from her and his father. Now Tolyan has to take care of her. Zheka doesn't expect to see him again until the morning. Tolyan opens and then locks the door of their room from the inside.

Zheka is alone.

Yulka steps out of her family's room into the darkness. Zheka runs down the corridor. There's music behind every door. The air is dark, and thick, and soft, and smelly. One of the doors is left ajar, and Zheka peers into the crack of bluish light: one of the neighbors is kissing his wife. Then another door, closer to the kitchen, opens a crack: a TV screen flickers, and an old bald man, Uncle Nikita, is brandishing his fist behind the screen. The music is getting louder and closer. Black turns to blue; the air smells like plums. Zheka stops. He knows that Yulka is near. He can't see her, he can only see into the place where the black is more black than just blue-black. She's breathing steadily an arm's length away, under one of the old bicycles hanging from the wall. He inches his way toward her in the dark. Now, finally, he can see her. She stoops, holding out her hands. He stands still. She moves. He steps back. She leans against the wall. He can see her eyes glistening where he thought she wasn't. She widens her eyes again. He jumps at her, pressing his lips hard into her face. She screams, jumps high into the air and hits him on the top of his head with her fists. He runs away from her and rushes into the kitchen, swinging his arms and shouting.

The kitchen is dark, too, although all the burners on the gas stove are lit, and all he can see are blue circles of flame floating like Christ's halo. His parents would be upset if they suspected that he knows this word: Christ.

Faina and two other old women stand at the open window, their faces blue. The music is very strong now, stronger than the chorus of cicadas in Sevastopol. People populate the windows in the building across the back yard. They eat, talk, laugh, move, cry, hiss, kiss each other. The world is so cozy, Zheka thinks the air probably could hold him. He runs up to the window and begins to jump. Faina grabs him by the suspenders on his short velvet pants before he's halfway out the window. Without a word, she pulls him back in, slaps him on the face, pushes him angrily to the door. He falls down on the floor. The old women shut the window, gasping and exclaiming excitedly. But he hadn't planned to die. He's no fool. He just wanted to rise into the clear night, that's all.

He races back down the corridor. His room is dark. He's still alone. His parents must have gone to his grandmother's, Auntie Aza's sister. Dima, no doubt, is with them, shrieking and babbling away.

Zheka peers down from the window. There's a flickering red dot of a cigarette above the invisible bench below: the man is still there.

Carefully stepping over the books and chairs on the floor, Zheka walks out of his room and, once outside, sneaks to the entrance door on tiptoe. Tolyan, too, is there. He grabs Zheka's arm from behind. Zheka spins around to face him. But he can't see his face. "Where're you off to?" Tolyan hisses. "What're you up to? You think I'm a fool? You're too smart for your own good, you know that? If I find out that you were pulling my leg, I'll kill you!"

"I really don't know what you're talking about, Tolyan," Zheka says. "Look, could we talk some other time?" He unlatches the door, noiselessly. "Ah," he thinks, running down the stairs toward the back yard, "life is very good!" And it is.

Dog Days

Melkovodje (Shallow Waters), a village in the Crimea, was separated from the mountains by a narrow river, also called Melkovodje, which ran parallel to the sea. The nearest resort town, Alushta, was fifteen miles away; it took a Meteor speedboat two hours to cover the distance between Alushta and Yalta. Sevastopol was farther west; Simferopol, the capital of the Crimea, was farther north. Early in the morning, a foreign coast was almost visible from the Melkovodje beach. Ayu-Dag, Bear Mountain, the bear lapping the salty water, protruded into the sea to the left. On its other side was Artek, the all-union summer camp for the nation's most distinguished teenagers. I had no hope of ever going there.

There was a set of wooden swings on the beach, five green wooden changing booths, and the "Magnolia" restaurant, where the local orchestra played music every night and all the waitresses wore short red dresses and ponytails. On my first night in Melkovodje I walked into the restaurant and sat in the corner by the window, watching the people and the orchestra. One of the waitresses, a tall redhead, glanced at me and smiled. She crossed to my table and told me that children were not allowed in the restaurant after dark and that I had to leave. Later, standing on the beach and looking at her through the open window, I wondered how old she was. She couldn't have been much older than twenty. She was taller than me, but I was growing fast, and when I was twenty, she would only be twenty-six.

That year's number one song in the Crimea was "Cheremshyna," Ukrainian for the bird cherry tree's sweet-smelling blossoms. It was sung in a dreamy voice verging on a sob. Ukrainian sounds almost like Russian, but not quite: I could only recognize every second word—"in the evening . . . in the garden . . . wearing some kind of shawl or something . . . Wait, girl, wait."

The Crimea had been part of the Ukraine for decades, yet people in Melkovodje still spoke Russian, albeit with a heavy southern accent disdained in Leningrad. Our landlord had that unpleasant accent, and so did his son, who was my age. They lived in a stucco hut with four rooms, five minutes from the sea. My grandmother, my younger brother, and I occupied one of their rooms. Two married couples from Kiev lived in the other two. Rent in Melkovodje was lower than in Alushta, and much less than in Yalta or Sevastopol, but the warm blue sea was the same.

Every morning Grandmother cooked breakfast in the kitchen outside the house, talking with the two Kievan woman. Then she and my brother went to the beach. The weather was always good. Often dolphins feeding in the shallows would leap into the air, and the smaller city kids with pale skin, unaware that there were no sharks in the Black Sea, would rush to the shore, screaming, "Sharks! Sharks!" Their mothers hurried to hug them. In the evening Grandmother would watch TV in the landlord's room. He worked at the local winery and never came home before midnight. His son, my brother, and I played soccer in the street in the afternoon.

Aside from the sea, the winery was the village's main attraction. It produced Massandra port, an export that was hard to find in big cities and was sold at the Magnolia, the only place to go after dark. It was my third night in the Crimea. The orchestra was playing in the night, drowned out by gusts of loud laughter, and the sea smelled of mussels rotting in the wet sand. There were specks of fire scattered along Ayu-Dag's back, and—miles and miles away—the multistoried ocean liners, slowly proceeding toward Yalta, Sevastopol, Odessa. I was standing on the beach, watching the restaurant door, hoping that the redheaded waitress would suddenly come out and begin to walk forlornly across the sand. Should she see me, I would run away. "Stop, young man! Don't run!" she would call out.

Instead of her, a tall drunken man in a beautiful white suit stood at the door. He slapped the janitor on the shoulder and, waving his hands, headed toward the sea. The orchestra stopped playing, and I heard the plaintive screeching of the swings a hundred meters away. The sea was quiet. The drunk waded into the water ankle-deep, kneeled, and then fell flat on his back. I ran over to him. His eyes were closed. Bending over, I smelled the sweet Massandra alcohol on his breath. I touched and pushed him. He hiccupped.

We were alone on the beach. I looked up. The moon was dough-fat in the sky. The stars were like white, well-washed kidney beans.

"Beautiful, beautiful moon!" he said.

"Get up! You can't stay in the water!" I said.

"Says who?" He opened his eyes and stared at me.

I didn't know what to do. He closed his eyes again.

I had never seen the moon so huge before. Judging by its size, any minute the tide might start rolling in. I leaned down and tugged at his sleeve: "I'm leaving!" He shook his head, blinked, and hoisted himself onto his elbows. I helped him to his feet and he walked unsteadily away. It was getting late; I knew that Grandmother would be mad, but it was the beginning of the summer and I wanted her to understand that we were not in Leningrad anymore.

I expected to find her in front of the TV, but she was in the kitchen, upset. One of our housemates seemed to have caught her husband kissing another woman from Kiev, the prettier and younger one. Now both of them were screaming at each other at the top of their lungs. "We're housemates and have to learn to get along!" Grandmother said to them. "Calm down! It's too late to start looking for another place." She was right.

The two women from Kiev had become enemies. After hours of silence in the kitchen—it was so small you couldn't help but touch another's elbow—they would spark with spite and start to spit, shove, and scream. They, too, had a heavy accent, yet I could understand what they said enough to be surprised and fascinated by the intensity of their mutual hatred. It was crude and shamelessly loud. As I listened, it occurred to me that people who could hate openly couldn't really hate and weren't dangerous, but I didn't care: I was scared. I didn't want to be around them, even if they hated each other simply because the kitchen was small.

There were mountains surrounding the town, none of them as high as Ayu-Dag. Climbing them wasn't easy.

On my fifth day in Melkovodje, I found a secluded place of my own up on the cliff overhanging the sea. No one could bother me there. I looked around. The sun was hot; it diluted

the color of the sea and bleached the sky. The air stood
between the sea and the sky like melted glass. It was filled
with the gnawing of cicadas. The bitter smell of worm-
wood and mint eventually put me to sleep. As I woke up
uneasily, my eyes half-blind with sharp pain, I saw the
breathless sun in the west and the old, silent Crimean women
walking up dusty paths, followed by dogs and goats.

On the way home, passing by the house across the street,
I glanced at its single window and saw a bloated face behind
the glass. It was a boy. I waved and nodded, but he never
looked my way. "What's wrong with him?" I later asked
our landlord's son.

He frowned: "The guy's been paralyzed since he was
born."

I thought about it. "Here, at the sea? What a shame!
One should be a paralytic someplace else!"

"There's more to life than just a suntan," he said. "That
boy reads a lot. He thinks a lot."

"I think a lot, too," I said.

"Well, keep thinking," he said.

He clenched his teeth. It seemed like he was getting
mad at me. "What's wrong with you?" I asked. He looked
away.

"Supper's ready!" Grandmother announced, opening the
door of our house. I was always hungry that summer.

After the last meal of the day, I went to the beach and
stood in front of the Magnolia until half past midnight, when
it closed. The sea was quiet, the orchestra was playing—
badly; the ocean liners' sirens drifted in like a slow wind
from afar. At one o'clock the redheaded waitress appeared
at the door, having already changed into a sarafan. She
crossed the beach and headed up the street. I followed in
the distance, watching her, all the way to the only apartment building in Melkovodje, hidden in the shadows of the

plane trees. She turned on the light in her room. I went back to the beach.

It had been a week since I'd left Leningrad. No one could see me in the dark. I was standing on the beach, looking at the open window of the restaurant. The orchestra stopped playing. The invisible wind had died down. During the lull I heard the swings. "Hey, you!" a girl's voice called. I turned around. There was a girl sitting on one of the swings. I paused. "Hey, you!" she said. "Come here! What are you—scared? Don't be shy!"

She had a nice voice with a heavy local accent. I came closer. She was about my age.

I said: "What's wrong with you? Why couldn't you come up to me yourself? Can't you walk?"

"I'm a *woman!*" She leaned back, gripping the ropes, tossing her hair, and gave me a smug look. She was pretty for a local girl. But then, she was the first local girl my age that I had met.

"How's Leningrad, Yevgeny?" she said. "I'm told it's bigger than our village!"

"A lucky guess," I said. "You must have asked my landlord's son about me!"

She stopped swinging. "You're intrigued; I know you are. I can see it in your eyes! Now go away."

I shrugged and left.

I thought about her. She was bizarre. "Who is she?" I asked our landlord's son. He told me that her name was Zinaida.

"That's a country-bumpkin name," I said.

"Not in Melkovodje!" he said heatedly. "We call her Ida. Ida's a nice name."

"It's not unsophisticated," I said.

He frowned. "Stay away from her." I felt that he was getting mad.

"I'm not taking any orders from you."

He lowered his eyes, but his face remained angry and stubborn. "She doesn't need people like you around," he said, looking away.

"Maybe she does," I said, wondering what kind of people I was.

"I'm warning you." He headed to the house.

"She's pretty for a local girl!" I shouted at his back.

We stopped talking. Playing soccer with my younger brother was no longer any fun. One afternoon I went to explore the outskirts of the village. I came to the tourist center, a shabby two-story building with rows of ping-pong tables inside. Two local boys were sitting on the rusty grass by the outer wall, one of them smoking. "Want a smoke?" he asked, looking at me. I shook my head. "I didn't think so," he said. We started talking. After a while we went inside and played some ping-pong. I was a better player, and soon we went back outside. I told them about Leningrad, its palaces and drawbridges, about the mighty and majestic Neva on a White Night, when no one sleeps, and Nevsky Prospekt, St. Isaac's cathedral, the Bronze Horseman. They listened with their mouths hanging open. "Close your mouths!" I said, laughing.

"What a life! You don't know how lucky you are!" one of them said.

"Of course I do!" I said. "Leningrad is Leningrad, it's not your Melkovodje."

"Melkovodje's not that bad," another boy said.

"Not bad?" I said. "What's not bad about it? What do people do here during the winter—drink?"

"And what do *you* do during the winter—go to the opera?" the first boy asked.

"I go to the movies," I said.

"Well, keep going," he said, and they turned away.

I went up to my place on the cliff. Almost there, I heard two laughing voices from behind the bushes. As I got closer I saw a man and woman kissing on a huge pink Turkish towel spread over the stones. I made one cautious step forward, trying to get a better view. A dry twig, one of the many that I'd scattered around for an approaching stranger to step on, crackled under my foot. The man raised his head, blinking against the sun. His face looked vaguely familiar. "There's someone out there!" he said. The woman laughed: "It's probably just a lizard or a snake!" Her face, too, looked familiar. "A snake?" the man yelled in mock horror. I rushed away, down the only path that led to Melkovodje.

Grandmother was in the kitchen. She told me to take my brother to the beach. "I'm busy watching two crazy women," she said, "and you don't even want to play soccer with your brother! You're beginning to make me angry!" My brother smiled coyly behind her back.

The beach was crowded. The dance music was blaring. The sight of hundreds of tanned people cheered me up. I sat on the sand and listened to the bantering of the nearby card players. One of the voices sounded familiar. It was the drunken man who had almost fallen asleep in the water the other night. He couldn't be more than twice my age. I walked up to him and said: "Hi! It's me!" The players studied their cards. I just stood there.

Then he glanced up. "Are you a good boy or a bad boy?"

"I don't know," I said. He didn't recognize me.

"Go make up your mind and come again."

I nodded.

"Semyon, he's just a kid!" another player said.

They looked at me and started to laugh.

"I'm leaving!" I said, and made a step back.

They laughed louder.

"A *Leningrad* kid!" said the man I knew.

"A lucky guess," I said uncertainly.

"It's your accent," he explained.

I thought about. I didn't know that I had a Leningrad accent.

There was no such thing as a Leningrad accent. Standing on the beach that night, I tried to imagine the distance between here and there. It was vast. After it had been decided that Grandmother would take me and my brother to the Crimea that summer, my classmates had said: "Lucky you!" Now I realized that it would be a long time before I came to the Crimea again. It had taken me fourteen years to see the Black Sea; maybe the next time I came here I would be twenty-eight, and then forty-two, and then fifty-six, and then my life would be over. But I wouldn't come to Melkovodje again, because life was too short to visit one place twice. Being here meant that I couldn't be anywhere else at the same time; it eliminated all other options. It was sad—to know that being somewhere, even once, meant unwisely using up my lifetime; that I hadn't yet found a wiser way to spend it; that this drab gray sand under my feet was unrepeatable; that someone else, within his own lifetime, would get to watch the Melkovodje waves. Then again, it was no big deal. I looked around. I had hoped to find Ida on the beach, but she hadn't come.

The orchestra stopped playing. I heard loud laughter through the window. I turned to leave and saw the same girl I had seen on the swings limping heavily across the beach. I recognized her instantly. I could see, even from the distance between us, that she was slim and pretty. She stepped carefully. I could hear the creaking of the dry sand. The diminishing moon was above the sea; dark, grinning shadows shifted across its surface. I didn't know what to do, where to hide. I turned away and counted to ten to calm myself. Then I laid down on my stomach in the gray sand. I wished I could dig myself deep, deep into it. But, of course, I knew that digging deep into the sand was no solution. The

girl wore a heavy, awful-looking shoe on her left foot. I knew
that she might have noticed me. The orchestra started
playing again. I got up and ran from the beach.

At home everyone was watching TV, together for the
first time in days. They stood silently in front of the black-
and-white screen, as if caught in mid-fight. Even my younger
brother was there. A cosmonaut was hopping clumsily along
the rocky white surface. He looked like a wind-up toy.
"Sh-h!" Grandmother said as I slammed the door shut.

"Just leave me alone!" I said, although no one was
looking at me.

"Sh-h!" she said.

"The Pentagon has already declared its intention to use
the surface of the Moon for the deployment of a new gen-
eration of strategic missiles, thus taking an unprecedently
dangerous step up in the arms race," the late-news anchorman's voice said. There came another voice, distant and
muffled, filtering through the crackling sound of the dis-
torted picture: "It is a small step for me as a man, but it is
a gigantic step for all the people of the Earth." Then, after
a pause, the anchorman announced: "This is a historic
moment. American cosmonaut Neil Armstrong has just
delivered his first message from the Moon."

"Isn't it nice?" Grandmother said.

"How come he was speaking Russian?" I said.

"Who?" she asked.

"The American!" I said.

"Sh-h!" she said.

When the picture disappeared, for a moment everyone
stood motionless. Then they went to bed. Far away, at the
beach, the orchestra was playing "Cheremshyna."

The same group of card players was on the beach the next
morning. The one who hadn't recognized me yesterday,

Semyon, was among them. He wasn't looking at me. "There's a man on the Moon!" I shouted, waving.

"Anyone I know?" he asked.

"An American," I said.

He nodded grimly. "Damn!" I realized that he was mad at me. My heart sank.

"I thought you had a jack," he told another player, and he got up from the sand. "I just hate playing with dilettantes!"

I shielded my eyes against the radiant sun with my hand and saw Grandmother and my brother in the sea. She couldn't swim and he was teaching her.

The man turned to me.

"What's your name?" he asked. "Don't lie. No, wait, let me guess. Is it Alexei? No, it must be Mikhail! Am I right?"

"It's Yevgeny," I said, smiling guiltily.

"What a coincidence! I'm Yevgeny too! We're namesakes." He put out his hand. I shook it.

"Stop it! Stop it!" I head Grandmother shriek. My brother had let go of her where she couldn't touch bottom.

"I thought you were Semyon," I said, and smiled, inviting him to laugh at my stupidity.

"You were wrong," he said.

"Semyon, are you still playing or what?" one of the players asked.

"Yevgeny!" Grandmother called out, noticing me. "Come swim with us! It's *heaven!* You have to spend some time with your brother!"

"Who's that old fishwife? Your granny?" he asked.

I shrugged. He stepped back, picked up a tote bag from the sand, and pulled out a green bottle of beer. "Care for a sip of beer, namesake?"

I shook my head. Grandmother had finally come out of the water and was approaching us. She looked young. The man chuckled.

He noticed that I was looking at a thick magazine wrapped in a newspaper inside his bag. "From one man to another," he said, pulling it out. "Take it. It's for adults only! You'll have to give it back, though. Don't lose it."

On the magazine cover was a half-naked woman. She was posed covering her breasts with her elbows. The only thing she had on was a necktie. My heart skipped a beat.

"It costs a lot of money," he said.

I gulped.

"Don't you want to introduce me to your new friend?" Grandmother asked as she came closer.

He laughed and slapped my shoulder. "Let me guess!" he said to her. "You're Yevgeny's older sister!"

She beamed at him.

I walked away.

I wished I had been able to read English. Although I had already started studying it at school, I only knew the alphabet and a few words. The name of the magazine just didn't make much sense. I knew the word "boy"—*malchik*—and "to play"—*igrat*. Together they sounded like a command for a dog: "Play, Boy!" "April," no doubt, was *aprel*. 1969 was 1969. I was alone up on the cliff in the Crimea, getting ready to open a magazine for men.

I went through the list of names on the cover. One of them looked Russian: Nabokov. I wondered: how did a Russian get to America; how come he was writing in English? His story in the magazine occupied dozens of pages. It was called "Ada," which was my uncle's wife's name. I had never seen a photo of a naked woman before—only paintings and sculptures in the Hermitage. The sun was hot; my head was reeling.

The stones were hot too, and sleep was like sunstroke. When I opened my eyes, crowds of black insects were dancing in the sun. A lizard was sitting on the stone next to my head. I lifted my numb hand and then lowered it slowly, preparing to cup the lizard in one swift motion. It must have sensed the change in the stillness of the air and slipped off the stone. My palm hit the hard rock. I jumped to my feet and stepped into the tall weak grass at the edge of the cliff. The lizard rustled in front of me. I bent over, looking for it, and glanced toward the sea. I almost lost my balance. In the shallows, rocks were embedded in the sand. A loud sound, even a puff of wind could bring me down. The dry dust and granite particles began to trickle down from under my feet. I imagined myself falling, my arms and legs flying clumsily in the air. I wondered if the lizard had miscalculated the limits of its world and had fallen, like a weightless twig, into the sea. If it and I were to fall from the cliff simultaneously, we would, according to Galileo, hit the surface of the sea at the same time. I sat back down on the stone and looked at the magazine. I knew I couldn't take it home: either Grandmother or my brother would find it. I hid it under the stone.

On the way home I stopped, suddenly unable to breathe. I checked my pulse: my heart was strong, it was steadily pumping blood. Still, I felt light-headed and queasy.

The front door of the house across the street, where the paralytic lived, creaked open. Ida stepped out onto the porch. She was smiling. I looked away quickly. The smile looked silly on her face.

"I saw you last night on the beach," she said. "You pretended you didn't see me."

I shrugged.

"You didn't want to see me because of *this*," she said contemptuously, pointing at her thick black left shoe. It was glistening in the sun. Both of us stared at it.

"Ida, don't get mad. Let's be friends!" I said.

She was silent for a moment. "I'm not Ida, I'm *Lida*. So I was right: you *are* interested in me!"

"Lida is a country-bumpkin name," I said uncertainly.

She laughed. "You can say whatever you want now. You're interested in me. I *know* you are."

I thought about it. Of course, there was something odd about her. I had never met a cripple before, for one thing. All the people I knew were normal. They didn't win lotteries, but they didn't have cancer either. Their life was neither a matter of luck nor of its lack. The fact that both she and her brother were cripples was against the law of averages. "How come your brother's a paralytic?" I asked.

She laughed again. "He's not a paralytic. He's retarded. He looks like a man, but he's a child."

"Not a child—an idiot!" I thought.

Soon the evening came.

It was still early when the orchestra stopped playing at the Magnolia and several well-dressed people rushed out. Crossing the beach and looking at us in the lackluster glow of the moon, they shouted something, waving their hands.

"Oh my God!" she said. "Not again!"

"What's going on?" I asked.

"A dead dolphin at the shore!" she said.

The lights in the restaurant were dimmed; loud angry voices were heard. First the customers and then the members of the orchestra and the waitresses appeared in the door. The redheaded waitress was accompanied by a tall man in a white suit who was drunkenly hugging her from behind. The sound of a siren came from nearby. "Clear the beach!" someone with a nasal twang and a local accent said into a metallic megaphone.

"So much fuss over one dead dolphin," I said.

She gripped my hand. "It's a really bad omen. Now walk me home. I don't want to fall. Hold my hand tight."

No one could see me walking with her; the night was dark. She tried to step gently, favoring her left foot, to hide her limp. The more she tried, the more she failed. I thought I could smell the salty odor of a dead dolphin in the air.

"When a dolphin dies, it washes up on shore," she said. "After a while, it begins to rot and smell. Crimeans are very fond of their dolphins." She leaned her head on my shoulder.

"We can't walk with your head on my shoulder!" I said.

She sighed. "There's a certain magic in the air!"

Later that night, lying in bed, listening to Grandmother's wheezing and my brother's snoring, I couldn't sleep. The moment I closed my eyes I pictured the naked women from the magazine. I was afraid that I had gone insane and would never be able to think of anything else. That would be a disaster. I got up, put on my pants and shoes, and tiptoed out of the room.

The beach was empty.

There were stars in the sky and specks of fire on Ayu-Dag. I walked along the edge of the low tide, expecting to stumble over a dead dolphin's body. When I returned home, the sun was already rising in the east over Kerch and Feo-dosiya.

I fell back asleep.

Later, in the early morning, as I was walking up the street toward my place up on the cliff, a local boy, an eight or nine year old, stepped out from behind one of the fences and stopped me. "I've got a message for you," he said, spitting through the crack between his front teeth.

"What is this, a movie?" I said.

He glared at me.

I took the note, a folded piece of paper ripped from a lined notebook. Her handwriting looked touchingly child-

ish and provincial: "Love is in the stars, so don't be shy!
Your 'yes' can make me happy, your 'no' will make me cry!"

The boy was eyeing me with deep suspicion.

"Did you see the dead dolphin on the beach?" I asked.

"What dead dolphin? Tell me that you love her and
shut up."

"I was on the beach last night. The restaurant was
closed. People were running."

"An ordinary civil defense drill," he said, shrugging.
"Don't beat around the bush. Let's hear your answer."

He was even younger than my brother.

"How old are you—four? five?" I asked, and put my
hand on his shoulder. "How much is four plus five?"

"Is your answer no?" He spat again.

"I'm not giving you any answers," I said.

"Fine," he said. He spat again and walked away.

By the end of the day I was almost finished with the
magazine. As I turned the corner of our street, a round stone
hit me on the shoulder. I couldn't see who had thrown it. I
stopped and bent over, gasping. A bunch of local boys,
whooping with joy, jumped all over me. They brought me
down and started kicking me. I scrambled to my feet,
pounding the air, swinging my arms like a windmill. Once,
and then once again, my fist hit something, and one of the
boys screamed: "This dog bites!" Someone else said: "Bite
him back! Bite him *back!*" Then they ran away.

I stood there, trying to cry. My eyes were dry. I checked
my mouth: it was bleeding, but there were no missing teeth.
I couldn't open my left eye.

I had no other choice but to start walking again. Passing by the house across the street, I looked at Lida's retarded
brother's face in the window. It was so bloated and motionless that I couldn't imagine ever not being able to recognize that there was something wrong with him. I came closer
and saw my own reflection in the glass. My face looked slow

and sweating. It had been at least a week since I had last seen it: I washed my face over the kitchen sink every morning and never used a mirror in Melkovodje. I was disappointed. I had expected my face to look more mature. Whatever I knew about life didn't show on my face. It was bruised and bleeding; I couldn't let Grandmother see me.

I stood in indecision for a minute. The gate opened behind my back and I turned around. "I warned you," said our landlord's son, looking away. "You're not in Leningrad anymore!"

He sounded like a movie character.

Then he smiled shyly: "You weren't that bad, though. You loosened a couple of their teeth! You were good!"

He wasn't mad at me, after all.

Still, I needed to get out of this place.

"Could you tell my Grandmother that I'm spending the night at a friend's house?" I said.

He nodded. "Does she know that you don't have any friends here?"

"No," I said. "She doesn't. But she doesn't care."

"How very tragic!" he said. We stayed silent for a moment.

"One night won't help you much," he said. "I'll try not to hit you so hard next time."

"Don't do me any favors," I said.

He shrugged.

I had a ruble in my pocket. Two hours later I was in Alushta. Although it was a tiny town, after Melkovodje it looked like a big city. I walked along the streets, alone in the night for the first time, dizzy with the smell of tobacco flowers and magnolias. Tall young men in white shirts floated in out of the darkness, silent, flashing their cigarettes, smiling. Women were laughing. A smiling old Georgian was grilling shish kebab in the street, a ruble a plate. Sparkles flew around his head. I was hungry, but I only had fifty kopecks left. The sirens of the ocean liners were louder and clearer in Alushta. People were singing, children were running around; it was two-thirty in the morning, and the streets looked like a quiet celebration of a never-ending Friday holiday; like life the way it was meant to be. A young woman was standing on the street corner, busily hitching up her skirt and straightening her stocking. I couldn't understand why she was wearing stockings in the Crimea. She raised her head and said: "Stop staring at me!" I looked away.

Early in the morning I went to the Alushta beach, watched it slowly fill with people, and fell asleep. Then I took a passenger ferry back to Melkovodje.

The sea was light blue in the distance, and dark green, like a beer bottle glass streaked with the boiling foam, beneath the keel. I felt thirsty and hungry. I looked around. The passengers were reading newspapers and eating, their children were screaming at the sudden leaps of dolphins close to the boat. No one noticed me. These people must have saved money for years to get away from the dreariness of some obscure town in the Ural mountains and come to the Crimea, and now that they were supposed to be having the time of their lives, feeling the warm salty sea drops on their skin and gazing at the green mountains of the Crimea, they were simply reading and eating, looking purposeful and businesslike, as though more important things than the sea awaited them at the end of the boat trip; something besides getting older and dying. And yet, they were not mad at me, or at each other.

An old, overdressed woman on the bench across from me was eating ham and drinking lemonade from a bottle. I tried not to stare at her. She raised her head and frowned. "Are you hungry?" she asked. I nodded. She smiled: "Look at you! We've been in a good fight, haven't we?"

I nodded.

"Where're your parents?" she asked.

"In Leningrad," I said.

"You're too young to travel to the Crimea alone," she said. "When was the last time you ate?"

"Yesterday," I said.

"That's a shame," she said, finishing the ham. "You have to eat a lot, because you're growing and your body needs meat. You're going to be a man one day, you know that?"

I nodded.

"That's so exciting," she said.

It was still early morning in Melkovodje. Grandmother was mad at me: "You're grounded forever, young man!"

"I'm sorry, I'm sorry!" I said.

"He got beat up by the locals!" my brother said gleefully. I waved a fist at him. "I know all about you!" he said.

When I left the house, the street was empty. Turning the corner, I saw them, ten or fifteen local boys. They were standing in my way, waiting and grinning. "That place up there, where you're going—it's called Screwdome," one of them said. "Want to know why?"

"Let's get it over with," I said.

They were still, grinning. "What are you talking about? We don't fight ten against one," the boy said.

I passed beside them, trying not to bolt. They jumped me from behind, brought me down, beat me up, and ran away. It took me a minute to get up. One of them had kicked my left shin so hard that I could barely walk. Limping, I climbed up the cliff. My place had been visited by strangers. The magazine wasn't where I had hidden it. I sat down, feeling the drying blood on my face tightening the skin at the mouth. The day was hot and hazy. When I looked at the sun, it didn't hurt my eyes. I sat there; then I fell asleep.

That night the orchestra was playing on the beach, and

the sea was quiet. My birthday was eleven months away.

"Hey, you!" she said from the swings. "I didn't notice you!"

"You noticed me," I said, coming closer.

She giggled. "It's so dark tonight. Poor boy!" She touched my face. "Did they hit you hard? Monsters. Then again, it's not always wise to reject the one who likes you. Look at you: you're *bruised!*"

"Cats have good night vision," I said.

She laughed. "I don't need eyes to see your pain."

There were campers sitting around bonfires on Ayu-Dag; the ocean liners slowly proceeded toward Yalta, Sevastopol, Odessa.

"You're sick!" she said. "Where did you get that magazine? Those women, they're whores, they make me sick!"

"Give it back to me!" I said. "You're ruining my life."

She laughed again. Her laugh was shrill. "We're taking our life very seriously, aren't we?" She took my hand and stared at my palm. "You have a long life line. You also have a strong love line."

It was dark, but I could see that her eyes were closed. She wasn't beautiful: just pretty; not even pretty—beautiful. Pug-nosed and mysterious. I wished I could make her cry.

"You're shaking," she said. "Have you ever kissed anyone?"

"No," I said.

She laughed again: "Shut up. Don't lie."

I bent over and kissed her. It felt strange. I almost remembered having done this before. She sighed. "Now we're boyfriend and girlfriend. We'll never be separated! We'll die on the same day!"

"Don't talk," I said. "Just don't talk." I kissed her again, trying to hurt her. "You're *biting!*" she gasped. She clasped my head with her hands. She was strong. Her hands were hurting me. The orchestra stopped playing, the moon stopped glowing and, falling in love, I knew I was doomed until the end of my life.

Wings

A big country is a conductor's nightmare. It's full of passengers, and passengers are strangers. In August, when even in Leningrad the nights get longer, all you can think of is Edita Pyekha, a Polish-born star, singing "August. Autumn is near" from dawn to dawn over the train radio. You are young and sleepless. The road is endless. All you want is to be alone. You're tired. No stranger is a good man in your car.

In August, in the final week of our summer as assistant conductors, we were headed south, for Kishinev. I had little to do and nothing to write down in my diary. My only passenger since Leningrad, a middle-aged man en route to Vitebsk, had been sitting in my "Employees only! Conductor on duty!" compartment for the last four hours, drinking vodka and making politically dubious statements. I listened, nodding. His big mouth could have gotten him in trouble had he not immediately recognized an intelligent and decent person in me. As soon as he ambled off to the bathroom, leaving his jacket lying on the seat, I checked his jacket pockets, looking for his ID. I found it. He was not a journalist, as he had told me.

His occupation explained the emptiness of my car: he had reserved the entire car for himself. When he returned and began to open another bottle of vodka from his briefcase, I told him that I wished I were a journalist too. What could be more interesting than traveling all over the country on assignments, interviewing officials, fighting the injustices of life! He only smiled at my youthful naiveté. "Don't burn yourself, my luna moth!" he said, and put his hand on my shoulder. "Journalism is not for the inexperienced! Sometimes I'm forced to write shameful lies. My wife has left me because I'm always traveling, never home. When people learn I'm a journalist, they often won't open up for fear that I might write about them in my paper. It's very hard. Someone like you would easily find his ideals shattered by the roughness of real life!"

"I agree," I said. "But at least you can travel in empty cars during the summer season rush! Your editor must have taken care of that."

He gave me a suspicious look. His eyes were shrewd. My eyes, on the other hand, were sincere. He smiled again, reassured, and said that some privileges came with the territory. Good and important journalists, indeed, had whole cars reserved for them from time to time. But so what? It was no big deal. I might deserve it, too, one day. In the meantime, he wanted us to become good friends—why not? He wished he were eighteen again, like me.

"Dream on!" I said. "My grandfather looks younger than you!" We laughed.

We proceeded slowly across the Pskov region. The sun, surrounded by the pink haze, was about to set behind the western horizon. He kept drinking without getting visibly more drunk. I had met his type before, a meaty-faced breed, preserved in alcohol like permafrost in subzero temperatures. Our head conductor was one. Never fully sober, she still managed somehow to appear clear-headed. Yet everyone was aware of her gloomy private nightly libations.

It had been hours since I'd last thought about our head conductor. I looked at my passenger, who was staring dully out the window, his head propped on his hand. He was a tall, well-fed Russian in a three-piece suit. His elbow kept slipping off the table. His bottle was empty. I looked at a briefcase by his feet. We had already crossed the Byelorussian border and were two hours away from Vitebsk.

"What time is it? I need more booze!" he said, yawning. "I know you have it hidden somewhere!" He wagged a finger at me.

"You're already drunk," I pointed out.

"That's nothing!" he said. "I can take in more booze than there's blood in your body!"

"I don't know if I can trust you, comrade," I said.

"Oh, come on!" He hiccupped. "I know you people aren't permitted to have booze, but if you run into some kind of trouble, we'll protect you."

"We?" I asked.

"Our newspaper," he said.

An hour later, drunk, he fell asleep, snoring, his mouth agape.

I woke him up in Vitebsk, the city where Marc Chagall was born and where he began painting his flying Jews. The man's eyes were bloodshot. "Don't forget your briefcase!" I shouted in his ear.

He looked at me uncomprehendingly: "What?"

"Hey, you! You're a scumbag!" I said, slapping his shoulder. He smiled. I pushed him in the back. His head tilted back.

"Your briefcase! Don't forget it!" I repeated.

"Likewise," he said. He would fall back to sleep in whatever car awaited him.

I watched as he walked unsteadily away. By the time he awoke we would have already arrived in Kishinev, capital of Soviet Moldavia.

I returned to my car and found his briefcase still sitting on the floor in my compartment. I opened it; there were some papers inside. Suddenly the car was full of new passengers. It took me twenty minutes to accommodate them. They wanted tea. I served them and got five rubles richer. Then I asked them if they needed blankets—not yet— and made an entry in my diary. Twenty minutes later, passing by the head conductor's door in her car, I heard outbursts of rowdy laughter. She was inside with one of the railroad inspectors. I tapped lightly on her door, just in case. Of course, she could hear nothing. I stood there for a while, thinking, my diary under my arm. Three hours later we were in Kalinkovichi, a small Byelorussian town.

As we approached the station, I saw a barefoot Kalinkovichi girl leaning easily against a Byelorussian tree in the dusk. I had seen her four times before, twice in June and twice in July, for only a few minutes. She was my age. I could fall in love with her. I didn't know her name, though. We were ten meters away from each other. I hoped she could read the romantic insignia on my drab green uniform, below the little brass wings, the railroad emblem: "Leningrad College Students' Railroad Summer Training." "I'll be back!" I shouted. It was a lie. I knew I would never see her again. Our two August minutes in Kalinkovichi had expired, and I waved a take-off flag to the engineer. Soon it grew dark.

The night was soft and fragrant, and my comrades and I were in serious jeopardy. Our head conductor had outdone herself. She had stolen my diary. It had to be her: no on else could sink that low. She had seen me writing something in a thick notebook day after day and apparently didn't like it. Now she had plenty of evidence against us to present to the College Party Committee.

Late at night we had an emergency meeting. All of us, the temporary assistant conductors, were there.

When I told my friends what happened, they only shook their heads in disbelief and rolled their eyes. "Why did you, an intelligent person, need a diary?" they said. "It's so sentimental! A diary, for crying out loud!"

"Maybe I'm going to be a writer!" I said. We laughed.

Sasha K., whose car was next to mine, suggested we simply throw her from the train. "She's forfeited her right to stay alive!" he exclaimed. "She's humiliated us enough! She's so drunk all the time, they'll think she fell out by herself!" There was silence. Then I asked him if he knew how it felt to kill a human being. "No!" he said. "But it's been done!" I noticed that Veronica S. and Vitya N. were looking at each other. I thought it was strange.

It was my turn to speak. "I know what you're thinking," I said. "You're scared. When she presents my diary to the College Party Committee, they won't listen to us, they'll listen to her. After all, she belongs to their world. She's one of them. Is that what you're thinking?"

They nodded gravely.

"That's what I'm thinking, too." I said. "But listen, we're all members of the Union of Communist Youth, aren't we? We're their future! What harm can they do to their own future?"

"We don't know. *You* tell us," said Dima L. "We haven't read your diary, Yevgeny. If it's bad, they could easily kick us out of college."

"You personally have nothing to be afraid of," I assured him. "I don't believe I even mentioned your name once in my diary."

He brightened. "That's good!"

We were sitting in his car, the emptiest one that night, all twenty-four of us, thinking sad thoughts. The train, all twenty-four of its cars, was closing in on Ovruch, our first Ukrainian stop. Vitya's hand was on Veronica's shoulder. I thought that was odd since Veronica and I had almost spent the night together five hundred kilometers ago, near Pskov, during the last trip, and I believed that it had meant a lot to both of us.

Veronica cleared her throat and said that she had overheard the head conductor, passing by her door two hours after Vitebsk, telling the railroad inspector, with whom she was drinking, that now she had that whole bunch of little intelligentsia kikes in her pocket. She giggled. Yura T., our team leader, winced at the word "kikes." I noticed that Inna F. was smiling at me. I thought that she was more interested in Venya D., who was tall and dark, and handsome, and maybe she was.

"Kikes, huh?" Yura T. repeated angrily. "Well, I'll show her!"

"Oh, shut up, Yura!" I said.

Not all of us were Jewish, like me. There may have been a handful, but we had no way of knowing. Only the head conductor knew our nationality, yet to her, we were all the same. Yura T., our leader, perennially gloomy, also knew, since he had seen our papers, but he refused to talk about it. I knew that he was Jewish himself.

Venya, smiling self-confidently at Inna, got up from his cot and turned on his cassette player. The only tape he had was Paul McCartney and his new group's "Banotherun." It was of very poor quality, had no label on it, and none of us knew enough English to make any sense of the title. We suspected that we weren't getting it right. Every time we heard Paul McCartney's voice, it reminded us that the Beatles no longer existed. Somehow it felt like a betrayal, as though they had finally surrendered to the thinly veiled hatred of our newspapers and TV, our head conductor and the College Party Committee. It felt pretty bad. But on the other hand, to make things a little easier for us, we were also free to think of Paul McCartney as just a jerk, one of them, who had nothing to do with us. Did it matter? No, not really. But then again: yes, it did.

In the night, as our train crossed the Ukrainian border, we started dancing, all of us, getting carried away in the limited space between the cots on both sides of the aisle. Since there were sixteen boys and eight girls among us, eight boys had to dance with each other. I was dancing with Inna, and Vitya N. with Veronica. We tried to rock and sway in sync with the train, letting go of our partners to clap our hands at the refrain, joining in with Paul McCartney's lead: "Banotherun!" The light in the car was bright and yellow. Our train was moving fast. The Ukrainian night was boundlessly, Gogolesquely black, and had anyone been standing atop one of the dark, smooth, mellow hills outside, he could have seen us, twenty-four boys and girls in green uniforms, dancing in the yellow bowl of light, clapping our hands and opening our mouths silently now and then, skimming over land without ever touching it with our feet, headed south in the late summer.

Early in the morning we were in Kotovsk, our last Ukrainian stop. It was a tiny town. I jumped off the train with two empty buckets in my hands. Old women with prunelike faces were selling cheap cherries, apricots, and peaches on the narrow train station platform. Soon I had my buckets filled with apricots and peaches. They cost me a ruble.

As I had almost expected, Veronica and Vitya had gotten off the train together. He bought her an ice cream.

The sun was everywhere. Even the beggars on the platform seemed to be having a terrific time in Kotovsk. They pushed and shoved each other good-naturedly, laughing, speaking in a staccato mix of Ukrainian and Russian. Green mountains surrounded the town. I thought: "This is my country." I was fifteen hundred kilometers from home.

I stood in the middle of the platform, eating a peach, in front of the bronze bust of Grigory Kotovsky, the namesake of the town and a legendary cavalry hero of the Civil War. He looked like a boulder with ears. I regretted not having my diary where I could attempt to describe the complex smell of corn, heat, drying horse manure, apricots, and peaches in the air.

Venya, the handsome one, stuck his head out the window and shouted something I couldn't hear against the laughter of the beggars and the old women's exclamations. I shrugged. He pushed his neck further through the window.

"The news!" he shouted again. "On the radio! They've just impeached Richard Nixon!"

"Who has?" Vitya N. asked. They were standing behind my back, his hand on her shoulder.

"The Americans!" Venya shouted.

"Big deal. Screw Nixon!" I said.

"Who's Nixon?" Veronica asked, widening her eyes. Her thin, childish voice was annoying. "Don't tell me you don't know who he is," I said. "Boy, you must be even dumber than you look!"

She shrugged her shoulders, and Vitya's hand slipped off one of them. He put it back. "Watch your mouth! You're talking to my girlfriend!" he said.

"For your information, 'impeachment' and 'peaches' sound alike in English!" said Venya, his head still in the window. I told him to stop showing off and shut up.

I saw our head conductor. Her drunken face was looming in the sun two cars away. Grinning, she looked at me. I turned around and picked up my buckets from the platform. Forty minutes later, as we were passing Bendery, I stood in the open door of my car, waving to a team of corn pickers, ten or twelve young and tanned Moldavian girls in red kerchiefs, smiling behind yellow walls of corn. "Don't get married before I come back!" I shouted. They saw me flying by with my mouth open. One of them shouted something in response and they burst out laughing.

That night, homebound, after an afternoon in Kishinev, I had only one passenger, a stocky man en route to Vitebsk. He had boarded the train a minute before departure and asked me if I had found a briefcase left yesterday by his colleague in my car. I showed it to him. "I was going to hand it to the department of unreclaimed items at the train station in Leningrad," I said. He said that I should hand it to him.

He seemed tense. I offered him a glass of wine. He declined.

I offered him a glass of tea. The night was muggy. He nodded. "Tea would be good. The night is hot," he said.

He took off his jacket and asked me if I had by any chance taken a look at the briefcase's contents.

"Oh, comrade, there's no capacity for idle curiosity left in me," I said.

"Nothing important in there," he told me, opening the briefcase and showing me a stack of papers inside. "Bits and pieces of some articles in progress, that's all."

"None of my business. I mind my own business," I said.

As soon as he stepped out of the compartment, heading for the bathroom and leaving his jacket hanging neatly from the chair, I quickly checked his jacket pockets, looking for his ID. I found it.

When he returned, I told him that I'd soon have my colleagues over for a discussion about our head conductor's behavior. Perhaps he'd find it interesting. She had stolen my diary. He was welcome to sit in, if he liked.

"Why not?" he said. "I'd love to. Maybe our newspaper

could be of use to you. Maybe we could even become friends.
Our newspaper is looking for young friends."

I shook my head. "Friendship is such an enormous word!
It's like a bright light, like a lamp, and I'm a moth drawn
to it!" I said. "I'm afraid to burn my wings! I feel alienated!
To tell you the truth, I don't believe in friendship with a
stranger, especially if he's older than me. How can I, comrade? I've seen so many dishonest people!"

He smiled at me. I offered him a glass of wine. He nodded.

"I understand you perfectly, my friend. Believe me, I
can share your anger and confusion. It's us against them.
Let's storm the barricades! The world stinks, it's a disgusting place, I know. All you need is love, love, love is all you
need! But all you really need is a friend. Maybe we could
become friends. Think about it!"

I shook my head: no. Journalists have to write lots of
shameful crap. They're not us. He's not us. He told me I
was wrong, he was us. I shook my head again.

We were sitting in my car, the twenty-two of us. I knew,
sadly, that Veronica and Vitya wouldn't come. The night
was dark and hot.

We drank many jugs of young Moldavian wine from
Kishinev. It was rosy, thick, and tangy. The journalist joined
in our conversation, laughing at our jokes, slapping his
knees. He tried hard. I asked Inna to sit next to him and
keep his glass full, because no matter what he had in mind,
he was safer being drunk. She said she didn't like him.

"I don't blame you, Inna," I said.

We started dancing. He sat drunkenly, smiling conde-
scendingly, kindly. Venya asked him if he knew any English.
He nodded and began translating the lyrics of "Banotherun," but the only words he could come up with were "if I

ever get out of here" and "if we ever get out of here."

"The tape's very poor," he said.

"Yeah, right! Let's blame the tape for everything!" we said.

I told Inna to invite him to dance. She shrugged. Dancing makes a drinking person more drunk, I told her.

"Oh, all right!" She tugged at his sleeve. He got up and started dancing, staggering and stumbling, and then plopped down on his chair, out of breath.

"Oh, to be young again! I feel like I'm eighteen again!" He slapped Sasha K. on the back: "Hey, Jude! Let it be!" We laughed, and someone told him that he was old enough to be our father.

"Me?" He was shaken up. "If *I'm* old enough to be your father, then just about anyone could be your father! That Beatle on the tape could be your father!"

We laughed again.

I asked Venya how old Paul McCartney was. Venya didn't know: maybe thirty-two, thirty-three.

"That's how old *I* am—thirty-three!" my passenger exclaimed. Sasha told him to shut up. The idea of having Paul McCartney for our father was bizarre. In that case, we could be our own fathers.

The man's lips quivered, and his face began to take on the stubborn, angry, gleeful expression of a teenager who had always been beaten and humiliated by his schoolmates. As I looked at him, it occurred to me that there was a ready explanation on his face for why he worked where he worked. "Inna!" I said. She put her hand on his shoulder and told him that we didn't mean to hurt him, that we didn't hate him.

"Yes you do!" he exclaimed, his lips still quivering. "Why do you hate me?"

"Because we don't know you!" we said. "Who are you? What are you? Are you one of us? No, you're one of them!"

I stood up and told them that he was a journalist.

"Journalists are scumbags!" Sasha K. said.

"Not all of them," I said. "Some of them are honest."

"What are you talking about?" the man said. He looked puzzled.

The car door slid open and the head conductor walked in. She was sober. She saw us drinking and told us to please continue. She had my diary in her hand, squeezing it hard. We fell silent.

Everyone looked at me. "When did you start stealing other people's diaries?" I asked her, trying not to sound too sardonic. "Do you call that civilized behavior?"

She grinned. "I didn't even have to steal it! Someone sneaked it under my door in an envelope! And you probably think of yourselves as friends! You're so hopeless to not even be able to notice a Judas in your ranks!"

No one believed her, of course. "Nonsense! You don't know what you're talking about!" I said. "What a pathetic lie!" Everyone nodded.

"Oh well," she said. "I don't have time to argue with you. I don't care what you think. So I've read it! Big deal! You don't like me? That's fine, because I don't like you, either!" She opened my diary and prepared to start reading.

I told her to read the last entry.

"As you wish," she said, shrugging her shoulders, and flipped through the pages. "I'm afraid she's going to steal my diary," she read. "She's seen me writing in it, day after day, and apparently didn't like it. She's a mean, brainless creature. When I look at her ruddy face with those beady eyes, I'm afraid I might throw up!"

She clenched her teeth. I could see surprise on her face.

"See how well I know you?" I said.

"You're so clever!" she said, sarcastically.

"That's right!" I said.

"I didn't steal it!" she repeated. "I swear!"

"Oh, give me a break!" I said. "Who do you think we are?" We laughed. She told Venya to hand her the tape. He glanced at me, as if to ask: "Should I?" "Let her have the tape," I said. "She's not going to have much use for it. We'll get another tape."

She put Paul McCartney's tape in her pocket. I noticed a wedding ring on her finger. I tried to imagine the man who had married her. I laughed, I couldn't help it. She gave me a malicious stare and began to read my diary out loud, lowering and raising her voice. She read slowly. She was a lousy reader. All my fears, all my insecurities, all my loves! All that bullshit. I looked around and met the quiet eyes of my friends.

"The Diary of Yevgeny L., Temporary Conductor. Day one. We'd left Leningrad in the morning. Odessa is the point of our destination. In the afternoon, I had some red wine with one of my passengers. He's an old, jovial man with bushy eyebrows that look like Brezhnev's. He seems much smarter, though. At least, he can pronounce most of the consonants. He gave me a ruble for the tea, three more for the blankets, and told me to keep the change. What is he, a Rothschild? I have a good feeling that this is going to be a highly rewarding summer! Then Veronica S. and Sasha K. stopped by on their way to our insipid leader Yura T.'s car. We all had some more wine. She's very beautiful, though dumb, and I'd like to sleep with her very much. And maybe I will. Who knows? This is going to be a long, long summer. As to Sasha K., he's just a harmless idiot. Soon we had more guests: Vitya N., Inna F., and Venya D. Vitya seems to be all right, not too bright. But pleasant enough, until he opens his mouth and puts everyone to sleep with his talk about soccer. Venya D. is quite good-looking, but boy, is he stupid! He and Veronica probably would be a perfect match. Unfortunately, Inna seems to be in love with him. What's

wrong with women? Can't they appreciate someone witty
and clever? When we had run out of wine, I went to my
compartment and got a bottle of vodka. I keep it hidden
under my pillow. We had been warned, of course, that if
we were caught red-handed, with even one bottle of vodka
in the car, we'd be kicked out of college. But hey, he who
doesn't take chances doesn't get to drink the champagne!
My passenger gave me ten rubles for that bottle. God, so
far I just love this job! Music, wine, girls, new people, and
the vast expanses of Russia! Slowly, slowly, the air outside
grew dark. I was getting drunk."

"Enough already!" I said. "We get the idea!"

Inna sat next to me. She put her hand on my shoulder.
I wished I could love her instead of Veronica.

"I don't think you deserve to stay in a Soviet college,"
the head conductor said, looking up from the pages. "I don't
think you deserve the honor of wearing those railroad wings
on your uniforms. I don't think the Party Committee is going
to take this so-called diary too lightly. Admit it, you have
lost."

Yes, we'd lost. We were genuinely upset. "Comrades,
I'm sorry that my stupidity has gotten all of us in trouble,"
I said to my friends, looking at the passenger. "This lesson,
as well as our own shattered future, will serve us right.
Sincerity and honesty don't pay off in the adult world. We'll
learn to be evasive and obsequious. We'll learn how to survive. At least, I will!"

My passenger stood up, crimson with all the wine and
emotion. "Don't give up!" he said, shaking his fist. He stepped
in front of the head conductor, snatched my diary from her
hands and handed it to me. Her sticky thumbprint was on
the cover. "Bravo!" I cheered. We uncontrollably began to
applaud.

When we quieted down, the head conductor pointed to
the passenger and asked me who he was.

"A journalist," I said. "An honest man. He's my passenger." She squinted at the glass of wine in front of him.

"If you don't get off the train this minute, I'll call up the militia in Ovruch to have you taken in for hooliganism and drinking on the railroad," she said. "I don't care if you're a journalist. You have assaulted a train official on duty. Look around you: none of these little bastards, with whom you have elected to side, is going to say a word in your defense. Get off the train."

He looked around. No one was looking at him. She was right. None of us was going to say a word in his defense. We were no fools. I told him we admired him and would always remember him, but our courage had limits: we were scared. He winked at me. Then he winked at our head conductor.

"Comrade, if I were you, I wouldn't rush to push a man from the train without first having found out where he worked. You might just end up getting arrested in Ovruch yourself!" he said.

She only laughed: "Oh yes, of course. Please, forgive my stupidity! I didn't recognize you, Comrade General Secretary Leonid Ilyich Brezhnev! Get out!" She jerked him to his feet.

Yura T., our leader, rose to his feet. "What you're doing is illegal!" he told her. "And I don't like it when you call us kikes, either!"

"Oh, shut up, Yura!" I said. "Let's not get involved!"

"That's right!" the head conductor said. "And what's wrong with calling you kikes?"

She walked out of the car. The next moment we heard the hissing of the emergency brake as she pulled it down. It was the first time anyone had stopped the train in our presence. We had been taught that only a fire justified pulling down the emergency brake: it took only six minutes for the inside of a moving car to burn out completely, and if the train was stopped, more than twenty minutes. She returned.

The train sighed and began to slow. She told my passenger to pick up his belongings and get out. He looked around, smiling uncertainly. He had drunk just enough to start feeling warm and friendly toward everyone. Then his face took on an angry, gleeful expression. The night was dark, but it was not unpopulated. We were only a couple of kilometers away from a small Ukrainian station. There was a telephone in the station office. By the time we were in Ovruch, he would have had enough time to talk with the Ovruch militia. I felt sorry for our head conductor. It was not her fault that she was so dumb. I walked up to her and offered her my diary. Everyone looked at me.

"Are you out of your mind?" she said.

"No," I said, "but my diary just doesn't belong to me anymore. It has your sticky thumbprint on the cover. Let it torment your conscience in the wee hours of the morning!"

She reached out to grab it, but I pulled back my hand: "I'm not out of my mind. Why would I want you to have my diary? Are you out of your mind?" Everyone laughed. My passenger slapped my back. He flung up his hands and made two V-signs. Everyone except the head conductor and I looked away. I stepped into my compartment and brought out the briefcase. "You almost forgot your briefcase!" I said.

"We are waiting!" she said.

He put his hand on her shoulder. "I'm not saying 'farewell' to you, I'm saying 'see you soon,' " he told her. She pushed him out of the car.

She returned and ordered us to get back to our cars. I told Yura T., our leader, as he was passing through the car doors, to quietly warn everyone that the militia would probably board our train in Ovruch, and that if anyone had stowaways, they should be dressed in our uniforms and look like us, because who could predict what the militia would be up to.

"Why?" he asked.

"Because now *I'm* the leader!" I said.

The train began to regain its smooth speed. I walked two cars down the moving train, to Veronica's compartment, and knocked on her door. There was no response. Then I heard hasty whispers, quick hisses, the rustling of bedsheets. I knocked again. "I need to talk to you!" I said. "It's important! Open up! I know you're in there!" There was no response.

I felt very sad, as always when a glimmering of hope turns into emptiness before me. "To hell with both of you!" I shouted. Let the militia find them in there, spending the night together.

I got back to my compartment and looked for a while at the thick darkness outside. Suddenly a strong fear made my heart sink. I started sweating. I got up. My legs were wobbly. I walked out, into the deafening metallic roar of the space in between the two cars, and pulled down the emergency brake on the wall. It went down limply, like a broken arm. The head conductor had already pulled it down. The emergency brake couldn't be used twice.

I returned to my compartment. There was a dying fire in the stove across the corridor. I reached out and shoved my hapless diary into its red-hot opening. I remembered that I hadn't slept for two nights and fell asleep.

I awoke just as the train stopped. It was still night. Outside, a dusty lightbulb swayed softly in the slow Ukrainian wind. Someone was banging on the door of the car. My head was reeling. My eyelids were heavy. But I knew what to do. We, the trainmen, had a cure for drowsiness. I picked up a pocketknife from the table and lightly cut my forefinger. Then I sprinkled the cut with salt from the box on my table. The pain, unbearable at first, subsided

in a moment. Now I felt miserable and angry. The air in
the compartment was sickening, it smelled like apricots and
peaches. Someone banged again. I heard the doors opening
in other cars. There were people outside. I got to my feet,
picked up my flashlight and flag, and went off to open the
door.

It was raining. The militiamen climbed in. There were
three of them. I pointed them in the direction of our head
conductor's car. "August. Flowers have withered," sang Edita
Pyekha from the station office. "And I know that you like
me, as I used to like you." Old women were selling baked
potatoes, boiled corn, and warm milk on the wooden platform. I bought a glass of milk, an ear of corn.

"Where's your home, sweet boy?" one of them asked
me.

"Leningrad!" I said. "Ever been there?"

"Are you going home now?" she asked.

"Yes!" I said.

"That's good!" she said.

There was loud talk coming from afar. I waved the take-
off flag to the engineer, but the train wouldn't move. I closed
my eyes and began counting to one hundred. Then I waved
the flag again and we took off, heading northwest.

A Room for Two

Heavy snowfall driving slantwise through the shifting cones of yellow light on the train station platform smeared women's faces with melting mascara. It was hard to keep one's eyes open.

A Leningrad man and his girlfriend, holding hands, stood in front of their car. They had been together two weeks.

His name was Yevgeny Litovtsev. He was twenty-seven years old.

"You seem pale," his girlfriend said. "I hope you're not coming down with a cold. That would be a shame."

The train shuddered and let out a low growl. They went inside.

All night the train worked its way westward.

It was still dark when an Estonian conductor slid their door open and walked in.

She said something in Russian. The sound of her accent woke him up.

He opened his eyes.

The air in the compartment smelled of stale champagne and bad breath. A warm back was pressed against his chest. Big powerful wheels were unstoppably at work underneath.

He felt queasy.

He raised his head from the pillow and lost his balance. His body slipped off the edge of the bunk, which was too narrow for two.

He thought: "This is the most embarrassing moment of my life."

He was sitting naked on the floor. His underwear were in the soot under the table.

The Estonian woman stared at him.

A Russian woman would have blushed and turned away.

"Tallinn," she said and pursed her lips.

He realized that she was waiting for a tip.

"Tallinn in ten minutes," she said.

This time her Russian sounded deliberately bad.

He nodded. She gave him an angry look.

The compartment door slammed shut. Two empty glasses rattled on the table.

His girlfriend yawned and stretched out on the bedsheets.

"Why didn't you say something in English?" she said.

"She's such a fool!" he thought.

Instantly he felt ashamed.

He was unwell.

He got dressed and walked out into the narrow corridor. It was full of people with the same gray towels around their necks as the one that he was holding in his hand. Men and women formed uneven lines to the two bathrooms.

The conductor was nowhere to be seen.

He thought: "She didn't even offer me tea!"

It grew light as the train pulled into the station. He

picked up their bags. He and his girlfriend headed for the end of the car.

His girlfriend stepped onto the concrete platform first. She turned to him and smiled. Her face was pink.

She looked, all of a sudden, like a girl he didn't know!

It was warm for a November day. The wind was wet. The air was filled with soot. He looked around. Seagulls circled the gray sky.

"Tallinn!" he thought.

The last time he had been in Tallinn was during his college summer naval camp practice. That was five years ago. Back then, he was a cheerful young man. Now he was overcome by nausea. If it hadn't been for his girlfriend, he wouldn't be here now. This trip was her idea.

They had met at the birthday party of a friend of his who lived next to the new hard-currency hotel put up by the Finns. That was a prestigious neighborhood. He remembered that night.

The crummy one-room apartment had been full of underground bohemians in jeans and turtleneck sweaters: writers, artists; freethinkers. She was there with a tall, athletic man in a suit. People grinned knowingly at the man.

"You may be one of *them*, but tonight, for once, we are *not* afraid of you!" their crooked smiles seemed to be saying.

The tall man paid them no attention. She stood amid the din, unperturbed. He had never seen her before. She was not a girl of his circle.

When the man, beginning to get drunk, went off to the bathroom, he smiled and winked at her across the table. She shrugged and frowned.

He felt likable.

"Where did you find that clown?" he asked her.

She said: "He used to be my boss."

"That's cheap!" he said.

She laughed. They started talking.

Before the man returned, they had left the party together. He hailed a cab. Soon they were at his place.

He had an apartment of his own.

They talked.

The next morning he thought about the man who had been her boss with glee. Then he realized that he should be feeling fear instead. Her former boss had to be a powerful man. Spending the night with his girlfriend might have been unwise.

She worked in one of the city's largest hard-currency exchange outlets run by the Special Service and knew many people whom he both feared and despised.

The very thought of those people made him feel angry. Yet she kept talking about them all the time. It was as if she believed that he, too, was bound to become a friend of theirs one day!

One of them, an Estonian man named Heino, manager of a newly built hotel for foreigners, had invited her to spend the November holidays in Tallinn.

Heino, too, had been her boss.

"Want to come with me?" she asked.

The idea made him nervous. He didn't like it.

It was dangerous. She knew it. He felt angry.

But *she* wanted to go!

They went to Tallinn.

Now the two of them were walking down the platform. They crossed the train station square and saw throngs of Russian tourists charging uphill.

The tourists were headed for the Old Town.

"The Old Town!" he thought.

Five years ago, during his naval camp practice, he had often come to the Old Town. It was an enchanted place.

Birds were always singing overhead. The air was redolent of the sea.

One night he got beaten up by several Estonian men. Something heavy hit him on the head from behind. He fell to the cobbles and threw up. His eyes filled with blood.

"You Russian dog!" someone said in bad Russian. "You go away! We don't want you!"

The men walked away.

He scrambled to his feet. His head was reeling.

Now he and his girlfriend were about to cross a street to their hotel. They caught their breath and paused at the red light. He saw a uniformed doorman.

The hotel was surrounded by a well-maintained empty space.

He and his girlfriend started toward the glass door.

She walked confidently. He trailed behind.

The doorman, making a forbidding gesture, stepped forward.

"Are you foreigners?" he asked.

She smiled and nodded.

"We're friends of Heino's!" she said.

The doorman waved. They entered the hotel.

It was clean inside. The carpet was plush. They walked into the elevator. Their room was on the nineteenth floor. She walked in and gasped. He peered in.

Their room was a small cubicle occupied by an unkempt bed. There were two chairs and an old black-and-white TV by the window. One could reach it without getting off the bed. There was no bathroom in the room.

A cracked enameled sink on the wall by the door was half filled with water.

She sat on the bed and sniffled.

"Heino promised me a *suite!*" she said.

He looked at her.

They heard footsteps outside. They were not alone on the floor.

He set their bags down and began to inspect the walls, one by one.

The walls were dirty.

He found a small round hole in the wall opposite the window, right by the bed's headboard. He stooped down, put his eye to the hole and saw a wooden bedstead several centimeters away.

The bed was now empty.

"Peeping Toms!" he thought. He almost smiled.

He could feel his face turn red. He, too, used to watch other people!

Years ago, when he was twelve or thirteen, he used to go to a public bath near school with the boys from his class.

There had been a back door to the bathhouse. They had a key to it.

They would unlock the door and sneak inside.

Cautiously, trying not to make any noise, they tiptoed down the dark corridor and peeked into the women's section.

There had been a hole in the wall.

Each boy had a minute. They took turns.

He remembered those afternoons.

Most of the time, all they could see were pink clouds of hot steam. However, once in a while a real showering woman would float into the field of their vision.

He turned to his girlfriend. She had already taken off her coat and her dress.

"I'm *bored!*" she said.

He sat on the bed next to her and reached out and turned on the TV.

The roar of Red Square burst into the room.

A tiny blurry picture emerged.

He saw thousands of faces, bobbing up and down, drifting past Lenin's Tomb.

The cameras focused on Brezhnev.

He was standing atop the Tomb.

His Persian lamb hat was pulled down to his eyebrows.

He waved his trembling hand.

"God, he's so *dead!*" his girlfriend said.

He turned down the sound and got up. His girlfriend fell asleep. He opened the window. It had begun to snow outside.

Humid Tallinn air filled the room.

He had never before seen Tallinn in November.

There were cathedrals and watchtowers everywhere.

Soon Tallinn disappeared from view. The horizon was covered with snow. He sat down on the windowsill and looked at the street below. It was still clearly visible.

The street was white against the black stone of the nearby buildings.

Down below, flattened by the distance, a short man in a black coat was slowly walking a large bird on a thin black leash.

The buildings on both sides of the street seemed uninhabited. The street was empty.

He shook his head and looked down again. The man was still there. He was blind. There was a flickering white cane in his hand.

He did have a bird on a leash.

It was a fat pigeon. The pigeon waddled through the shallow snow.

The snow drove through the air.

He glanced at his girlfriend. She was sound asleep. It was getting cold in the room.

The pair below began to cross the street. They reached the opposite side and disappeared around the corner. He laid down on the bed next to her and put his hand on her shoulder.

She shrugged it off and muttered something in her sleep.

He got undressed and kissed her. They made love.

The snow kept falling.

Some time had passed. He awoke with a bad taste in his mouth. He was thirsty, but his bladder was full. It was already dark outside.

The November days were short.

He rolled over on the bed and saw his girlfriend's face next to his. She seemed to be looking at him. The pupils of her eyes were glistening. She had short eyelids.

He nudged her with his elbow. She moaned.

He got out of bed and got dressed. There had to be a bathroom in the hotel.

He thought: "Maybe I could do it into the sink. She's asleep!"

He stared at the TV screen for a while.

Crowds were still marching past Lenin's Tomb. Brezhnev, feebly smiling, was still waving his hand.

"I hope this is a recording," his girlfriend said from the bed. She yawned and stretched out. "Poor old man! It's *cruel*, what they're doing to him!"

He turned off the TV. The room became dark.

Now no one would have been able to tell if they were here.

He could see nothing. "Are you there?" she asked.

They heard the door open in the room behind the wall. There were footsteps.
A man's voice said, in English: "I'm so tired! Oh God!"
She giggled.
The light went on on the other side of the wall.

He tiptoed over to the wall and put his eye to the hole.
A portly man with gray hair was sitting on a king-size bed. He was covering his face with his hands.
"What are you doing?" she whispered. "Are you out of your mind?" He waved her off.

They sat in the dark. His bladder ached. A vacuum cleaner whined out in the corridor.
His girlfriend got up from the bed and began to dress.
She crossed a weak beam of light jutting out from the hole in the wall. He saw that she had already put on the same dress she'd been wearing when they first met.
That dark light accentuated her beauty!

They heard the man's footsteps again. The door behind the wall banged shut. The man was gone.
She groped in the dark and turned on the light in the room. He blinked.
"Have you seen my belt by any chance?" she asked. "The gold one? Oh, there it is!" She picked it up from the floor.
At that moment the bare bulb overhead hissed and crackled.
The light in the room went out.
"This is just *miserable!*" she said.

He lay down on the bed and closed his eyes. A stab of pain through his heart made him wince.

He sat up. For an instant he was afraid he might be having a heart attack.

He waited. Soon his breath evened out.

His girlfriend went to the door. "I'm going to the bar downstairs," she said.

Gray, calm light poured in from the corridor.

She stepped out of the room. He followed.

The corridor was endless. They walked into the elevator.

"You don't have to go!" she said. "Maybe you should take a nap. You look ill." The doors closed with a hiss.

The doors opened. They were in the lobby again.

They turned right, turned left, and entered the bar. It was a hard-currency bar.

Loud foreign speech was heard. The bar was full of cigarette smoke.

The lights were dimmed. The music was soothing.

She walked in first. They crossed the crowded space.

Of course, because they were not foreigners, neither she nor he had the right to be here.

There was a bathroom in the bar.

"Where're you going?" she asked.

He saw his face in the bathroom mirror and was struck by its paleness. His eyes were pained. His lips were dry. His hair was wavy.

He liked himself.

He thought: "This man has been through so much!"

A middle-aged foreigner in a bulky sweater said something to him and laughed. He nodded.

When he returned, his girlfriend was sitting at the far corner table, looking at herself in a compact mirror and applying red lipstick. He sat down on the chair opposite her.

No one paid any attention to them.

She put the mirror back in her purse and pulled out two folded pieces of greenish paper. Each was the size of a candy wrapper.

She pushed one toward him with her fingertips. It was a ten-dollar bill.

He picked it up and quickly put it in his pocket.

He had seen dollars before.

"Go get yourself a drink," she said. "I just want to be alone for a while."

He got up from his chair and walked over to the bar. The lights in the bar began to blink. A shiny mirror ball spun overhead on a thin chain hanging from the wooden ceiling rafters. The music blared.

He smiled at the bartender and pointed to a half-empty bottle of brandy on the counter.

"One?" the bartender asked in English.

He shook his head and raised two fingers.

The bartender poured him two brandies. It cost four dollars. He had enough money to spend the entire night in this place.

A blond woman smiled at him from the other end of the counter. The music was now soft. The light was pleasant.

He bought another glass and looked at his girlfriend's table. She was talking with a tall black-haired man in a suit. He couldn't see the man's face.

He felt angry.

He finished his brandy and returned to the bar for another glass. Women were everywhere in the bar. He thought that it would be nice if he could try his English on them.

He would walk over to a strange beautiful woman's table.

He would start speaking English. Then he would switch to broken Russian.

The woman would think: "He's cute! He's a foreigner!"

He cringed.

It occurred to him that any local woman in this bar for foreigners only had to be a prostitute. Prostitutes knew English better than he did.

He would only humiliate himself.

"I'm such a fool!" he thought. He felt angry with himself.

He wasn't even drunk!

He could be pathetic at times.

Years ago he used to suddenly begin speaking English in the streets of Leningrad. He would ask people for directions, pretending he didn't know any Russian.

He imagined then that people were thinking: "He's not one of us! He's a foreigner!" But now he suspected that they'd thought he was making a fool of himself. His English wasn't good enough to sound foreign.

He took a big gulp from his glass and felt painfully ashamed of himself. What was wrong with him?

Dignity was not in his genes.

He liked that thought. He pulled a pencil out of his pocket and wrote it down on a napkin, in English.

In an instant he was flushed with filthy memories. The sordidness of his life amazed him!

He used to lie and cheat.

He stole money from his parents.

He told others his friends' secrets.

He had slept with his friend's wife.

He killed his *cat!* Bitter tears welled in his eyes.

The cat's name was Pushok: Fluff.

When a friend of his, drunk, had brought it to his house in a shoe box, it was so frightened that it wouldn't leave the box or try its voice.

Then, after a few days, it grew into a normal cat.

It had shiny fur and white paws.

One morning, when he was in an irritable mood, the cat started playing loudly with his slippers under the bed. He pushed the bed to the wall with his knees to show the cat just how mad he was.

As he slammed the bedside against the wall, he heard an abrupt gurgling sound. He quickly yanked the bed aside.

The cat was lying on the dusty floor with its eyes closed. It was still breathing. Black blood and pink foamy bile trickled out from its mouth.

The cat was still warm, but stiff, flattened by the bedside.

He picked it up and washed the blood off its face over the kitchen sink. Then he set it down on the mat in the bathroom.

The cat never opened its eyes. It didn't react to the stream of cold tap water. He thought it was dead.

When he returned home from work that night, it was still breathing. He tried to pry its mouth open to pour some milk inside. That didn't work.

The next day he called in sick and stayed home, watching the cat breathe and still hoping that it would somehow revive and start lapping milk from its plate.

Two days later he wrapped it in a newspaper, shoved it into a plastic bag, and took it down to the dumpster.

He was overcome with remorse.

He thought: "I shouldn't have been drinking." There was a pause as he was being eased into fear. The room darkened. The foreigners' faces blurred. The air in the bar was stale. It smelled of sweat and cigarette smoke.

He leaned up against the wooden wall. His lungs were

hurting. He steadied himself. His heart raced.

"What if I'm going to die?" he thought. He was ill.

He looked at his girlfriend's table. She was still talking with the tall man in a suit. They seemed to be enjoying each other.

She threw back her head and laughed.

He walked to their table.

She saw him. Her face took on the anxious expression. "You look *awfully* pale!" she said. He nodded.

The man she had been talking with gave him a lazy look. "What's up?" he said. "What's your name? You don't look like a foreigner. Do you have the right to be here?"

He only shrugged.

His girlfriend took the man by the hand.

"Oh, leave him alone!" she said. "Can't you see? He's not *feeling* well!" Her voice sounded as if it were coming from far off.

She leaned toward his ear and whispered: "Run!" He stared at her.

He couldn't run! That would be too humiliating.

"Wait a minute!" the man said, and grabbed his sleeve. "I can't just let him go. I want to see his papers first. Let me see his passport!"

He pulled out his passport.

The man opened it and studied the photo on the first page.

"Yevgeny Litovtsev!" he said.

He turned the page. His face expressed surprise.

"Interesting!" he said. "Look at this! Comrade Litovtsev has recently requested permission to leave the country! But we *can't* let him go just like that, can we?"

His girlfriend looked at him. Everything fell silent around them.

He thought: "How did he know?"

There was nothing about *that* in his passport.

The man put the passport in his pocket.

"It'll be safer with me," he said. "You can go now. I can't see your face. You make me sick."

His girlfriend fumbled in her purse and slid a key to their room in his hand.

"It'll be all right!" she whispered.

He turned around and walked away.

The bartender smiled at him and said in Russian: "No more brandy?"

A blond woman at the counter laughed.

He returned to their room and walked to the window. The Old Town cathedrals were like giant fishbones in the night. He turned on the TV.

They were still replaying the recording of the morning Workers' Parade in Red Square.

Brezhnev was still waving his hand.

He heard the door open behind the wall. Their foreign neighbor was back.

The wood creaked as a heavy body plopped down on the bed.

He turned off the TV and fell asleep.

The man's loud snoring woke him up. He felt furious.

It occurred to him that now, if his girlfriend were here, they would have to be discreet and silent, even though the man on the other side of the wall probably would not be disturbed by noises. Still, they would have to be cautious. He would put his hand on her shoulder and kiss the back of her neck. Sleepy and warm, she would turn to him and hug him. They would kiss.

It occurred to him that if she were in bed with him now, she would probably have already slept with the other man, and she would have come to him happy, tired, and bored.

There was no use thinking about it now. He could not understand why she had wanted him to come to Tallinn with her in the first place. Maybe she really did care about him and wanted the two of them to have fun! He sighed.

She was probably now trying to persuade the man down in the bar not to ruin his life. "Give me that passport! Please!" she probably was saying. Maybe she even felt forced to sleep with that man. Then again, that man probably had been her lover for a long time. He closed his eyes and tried to fall asleep.

If she were here now, she would have been asleep for a long time and he would be still awake, as always, staring at the dark ceiling, feeling uncomfortable. He could never get used to sharing his bed with someone. Usually, if he could not fall asleep for a long time, he would start nudging and pushing her lightly with his elbow, coughing loudly and sighing. He could never wake her up with his coughing.

He realized that he was falling asleep, thinking that when she returned he would not be alone in this room anymore and if something were to happen to him in his sleep she probably would know what to do.

The man behind the wall was wheezing and snoring. He banged his fist against the wall. The man continued snoring.

He rolled over on the bed and peeked through the hole in the wall. Now that his eyes were used to the dark, he could see the sole of a fat foot dangling from the bedside in front of him; the man was sleeping with his head pointed oddly toward the empty space in his suite. The noise was sickening.

He laid back down on the bed, found his jacket on the floor, fished out a pencil from the pocket, and, smiling, slowly pushed it into the hole; then he thrust the pencil all the way in, pricked the man's foot, and quickly pulled the pencil out.

The snoring stopped, the man said, "Ouch!" and turned on the light in his suite. Then he turned it off.

For a while everything was silent, until the snoring resumed, and the pencil slowly went into the hole again, but this time the man must have expected it. He had changed his position on the bed and was now facing the wall. His hand grabbed the pencil and quickly pulled it all the way in. "Son of a bitch!" said the man. There was a pause. Then the pencil appeared in the hole from the other side of the wall. He could hear the man's excited breathing. The pencil was sticking out in indecision halfway through the hole.

"What's your name?" the man asked, in a friendly voice. "Who are you?"

There was a silence.

He got up from the bed. A fresh wind from the open window calmed him down. Far away, the first cable car screeched along the empty streets. He began to get dressed.

He could still make it to a Leningrad train.

There was no use thinking about it now. He heard footsteps out in the corridor. They drew nearer, and then stopped. Someone was with his girlfriend out there. He held his breath.

What did they want from him? Why couldn't they just leave him alone? If they had come to laugh at him, he would slam the door in their faces.

Of course, he knew that he could do no such thing. He clenched his fists. If he could hold his breath long enough, maybe they would decide that he had already left.

After a while he realized that there was no one in the corridor. It was all his imagination. Still, he stood behind the door, waiting.

The wind outside had abated. An airplane roared across the sky. It was cold in the room. The foreign man snored on the other side of the wall. Some revolutionary music was playing.

It was still dark when the door opened. He was not asleep.

She was back.

Counterbalance

I'd left Leningrad so early in the morning that three hours later—and ninety-six kilometers further northwest—it was still early morning in K. It was pleasant, standing by the open train door, to realize that by the time most people were waking up or just leaving their homes for work I had already traveled a long way. It was also nice to know that I was sober. I took a final gulp of lemonade from the bottle.

I jumped off the train, an old and slow Zyelenogorsk transfer, and dropped my bag, heavy with canned food, on the dark creosote sand in front of the K. station office, a log cabin built by the Finns decades ago, when Karelia, that narrow strip of inland lakes and unobtrusive beauty, was still theirs. Now it was ours. Finland was three or four short hours away by train from K.—or could have been, had the local trains been permitted to stop in Finland. But, of course, they weren't. The area where the trains crossed and criss-crossed now was known as the forbidden zone. Thousands of border guards made up the bulk of its population. No one could enter the forbidden zone without a permit from the Ministry of the Interior. At some point down the road between K. and the next station, the border guards would board the train and check the remaining passengers' permits. I looked around: I was alone here. Nobody else was getting off at K.

The train sighed and shuddered. A large black-spotted dog sleeping on the porch of the station office twitched its ear at the metallic din. It yawned. Then the train started to crawl off, and everything returned to silence. I picked up my bag and headed down the soft dirt road of the hillside.

The sun stood very low above the treetops, striking blue sparkles off the lake glimpsed in between the trees. The forest on the other side of the lake was tall pine and fir, thick as a fence, green as the dark moss on its floor. The train let out a final, tiny squeal from afar.

At the station office, the black-spotted dog on the porch yawned and stretched, and then jumped on its feet, sniffing the air. I pulled a piece of bread out of my pocket and some sausage wrapped in a Leningrad newspaper, the leftovers of my early breakfast in Zyelenogorsk.

"Hey, Sharik, or what's-your-name! Polkan! Catch!" I said, tossing the sausage in the air. The dog caught it. Turning around after a few steps, I noticed that the dog was following me, and that it was a he. "Good dog! Good dog, Sharik!" I said, my voice strong and silly in the silence. He looked at me, wagging his tail. "No more sausage!" I said loudly and emphatically, as if he were a deaf foreigner. The dog yawned again, looking at me with amusing intensity. "Stop staring at me!" I said loudly. The dog wagged his tail a little stronger at the sound of my voice. "Dumb, dumb dog!" I said. He wagged his tail.

I walked away. The dog, baffled, yelped behind my back.

I looked around me.

Everything was blooming and blossoming, shooting up

on both sides of the steep hillside road. I stopped, full of joy, and knelt in the shadow of an old elm to smell little grasses and small, touchy, inedible mushrooms, blueberry and wild strawberry, violets. Everything was growing and sprawling, crawling with ants, and bugs, and beetles. For a moment I felt like falling flat, face down, right there, and then rolling over on my back and staying right there, in the grass and on the moss over the warm wet soil, my eyes closed, free and wise, patient, breathing freely, maybe even falling asleep, surrounded by kindness, unnoticed.

Soon I was in front of our house. It was half hidden behind the wire fence. I set my bag down in the tall grass and quickly smoothed my hair. My grandmother, the year-round master of our summer house, came up the red brick road between the trees with a bucketful of early August apples in her hand. She stopped on the porch and wiped the dirt from her galoshes against the rubber doormat before she went inside.

The next-door neighbor's Siamese cat, Maya, sneaking in under the fence, jumped onto the bench by the guest house, a plywood fantasy, my father's latest pet project. He had been doing a lot of building and rebuilding in the yard lately, on weekends: a bathhouse, a greenhouse, a concrete basement, a new foundation for the main house. His rapidly progressing obsession with construction work was now so fierce that it no longer even invited jokes about his losing weight, at last, and looking tanned, fit, and trim.

Maybe I should give him a call sometime.

"Maya! Hey! Maya!" I hissed from behind the front gate. The cat stared at me, her eyes sky blue. She was almost the same size now as when she was given to me, one distant day in May five years ago—hence, Maya—or when I had to get rid of her, two years later.

"Maya!" I called again.

The cat resumed licking her paw.

I unlatched the front gate, noiselessly. She jumped off the bench and dashed away. The smell of flowers, asters and gladioli, was stronger near the house. I paused. The cat stepped out of the bushes by the guest house.

"Maya! Hi! It's me, Yevgeny!" I said.

She looked at me with disdain.

I sat on my haunches and patted her. She began to purr.

"How come you didn't recognize me?" I said.

She rolled over on her back.

"Who are you talking with, Maya?" my grandmother asked from the kitchen. She couldn't see me, and I couldn't see her either. The cat yawned.

I stood up. The smell of flowers was all over me, like a warm wet blanket. I opened the door and walked in. My grandmother was still in the kitchen, waiting for a pan of milk to boil on the stove. "Hi!" I said, stepping behind her back. "It's me!"

She started.

When she turned around, there was a ready smile on her face. "You! You scared me!" she said. "I didn't expect you! I didn't know you were coming!"

"Do you want me to leave?" I said. She laughed and said: "Come here, let me kiss you."

I dropped my bag on the floor and leaned forward. She stood on tiptoe to kiss me. The times when she had been taller than me were now past. She looked old.

"Here!" she said. "Why don't you shave that beard? You look like an old Hasid!"

I noticed that the cat had jumped back onto the bench and was now watching the steam rising off the milk on the stove.

"She doesn't recognize me anymore!" I said.

My grandmother looked out the window. "Who? The cat? What do you expect from a cat?"

"She could've at least recognized the hand that fed her!"

I said. "Here, grandmother, I have some canned pork and a can of squid in my bag." I knew that she liked it when I acted like a real-world person. She smiled again.

"Good!" she said, pleased. "That's nice. It's been almost three weeks now since they had meat over at the station store."

"Our economy is a mess!" I shouted, stretching out my arms to throngs of impassioned listeners. She slapped me on the hand.

"Shut up!" she said, scared. "Are you crazy? Somebody'll hear you!"

"Hey, somebody!" I shouted. "Listen! Our *country* is a mess!"

"Shut up! Don't scare the cat!" she said. "How can you be so foolish? You're not drinking anymore, are you?"

"Who, me?" I said. "What are you talking about?"

"You're not leaving tomorrow, are you?" she asked.

"Oh no, I'm here for at least a month!" I said.

"Oh good!" she said. Then something crossed her mind. "Don't you have to go to work?" she asked anxiously. "It's none of my business, but aren't you still a public park night guard or whatever?"

"Of course I am. But I've decided to spend a month in the country, like Turgenev," I said cautiously.

"I see," she said, turning to the stove.

"I'm not in any kind of trouble," I said.

"No," she said. "I see."

"What do you see?" I said.

"That you're not in any kind of trouble," she said.

"That's right!" I said.

"I see," she said. "I see." But she didn't.

She didn't, and, much to my surprise, neither did I. Not any longer. Not since I had gotten off the train. The accumulation of eeriness in my life over the last weeks,

which had driven me out of the city, now seemed irrele-
vant, worth forgetting.

I'd dreamt it up.

There had been no anonymous phone calls in the middle
of the night.

Those two drunken faceless thugs—one tall, the other
short—who roughed me up, twice, at my doorstep, having
carefully put out the cigarettes they were smoking while
waiting for me: they never existed.

Still, I couldn't help wondering: what did they want?
They seemed to follow me everywhere, openly grinning at
me.

What was wrong with them?

Did they want me to go or did they want me to stay?
Did they want me to be dead or did they still need me alive?

My guess was that they needed me alive, yet nonexisting; invisible and weightless.

None of that mattered anymore.

"Okay, grandmother, brace yourself. The situation is
extremely grave," I said. "The house is surrounded by the
secret police. We'll have to fight. Do you have a gun?"

I winked at her.

"Shh-h, don't shout," she said, laughing too. "People'll
hear you! It just *looks* like there's nobody around!"

"Oh, grandma, why are you so scared all the time?" I
said, and hugged her. "Can't you stop being afraid? Wake
up, Stalin is dead! Look out the window: it's 1985, it's not
1951 anymore!"

"Oh yes? Is that so? *You* look out the window, then,"
she said.

I looked out the window. The yard was full of pale light
and golden apples. The grass was green. The bench was a
bench, was a bench. The cat was a cat. Grandmother was
right: the world was timeless. The lake was near. "Want to
go swim in the lake?" she said.

"Maybe; maybe not," I said, overwhelmed by my sudden freedom. If I wanted to I could go swim in the lake, or just stand, or sit, doing nothing.

"I'll go have a look at the lake," I said.

"Well then, fetch the bucket, get some fresh water from the spring on the way back," she said.

"I'll be *glad* to, Grandma!" I said.

''You're such a sweet boy!" she said, and chuckled. I knew that she was pleased I'd come.

It was pleasant to know that she was pleased with me. I smiled at her. I couldn't remember the last time I'd used the word "glad."

Halfway through the garden, toward the lake, I dropped the empty bucket from my hand. It clinked against the bricks, and the cat jumped off the bench. No one could see or watch me here. I fell to the grass, face down, and then rolled over on my right side. Now I was half-blind, half-deaf. The dragonflies and the bumblebees stood still in the ringing air over my upturned ear—a funny-looking, pale, waxlike funnel, a receptacle of insignificant sounds. My nose smelled the warm wet soil, the tall wet grass, distant water, the faint smell of slime in the wake of the trafficking earthworms. My left eye, now lower than the pointed tips of the grass blades, was contemplating the community of ants and beetles populating its tiny field of vision. My retina retained their bug-eyed images. I watched the bugs work. They were in a hurry. I blinked cautiously, trying not to scare them off. They looked content. They didn't seem to mind my presence at all. I knew that I could crush them with one finger, but they seemed to know I wouldn't do that. They knew that I posed no danger to them. We coexisted peacefully. We loved each other. My eyes welled with tears. The sun was warm, and the sky was blue, and the lake was near.

My heart began to beat tensely again; my impatience had destroyed the idyll. I got up off the grass, careful not to squash any of the insects as I headed for the lake.

Now that it was August, its shore was covered with a bright green rash of blossoms. The lake had grown more shallow, baring the drying silt and the forest of reeds around the narrow tongue of water that balanced our boat on its tip. But it was beautiful all the same.

I sat on the bench under the branchy lime tree. The bench and the tree itself always reminded me of Leo Tolstoy on his Yasnaya Polyana estate. He was a wealthy man and could afford the luxury of being a great writer.

I wasn't so lucky.

I leaned back and tried to start contemplating the matters of life and death, war and peace, balance and imbalance, finiteness and infinity.

No; I was no Leo Tolstoy.

Still, I felt good.

The lake, framed in furry firs, noble-looking stones, and granite boulders, was a placid sunny mirror, vintage Karelia. I closed my eyes. A slick green army chopper, preceded by its roar, flew in out of nowhere. It crossed the lake like a gigantic dragonfly, leaving in its wake only deafening silence. I noticed that there were several boats strewn about the visible part of the lake. The silhouettes of men, stooped over their fishing rods, stood bright and black against the sun. I watched them with envy.

Tomorrow, I told myself, looking at the lake, blinded by its radiance; tomorrow I'm going to get up at three or four in the morning, put on two warm sweaters and my thigh-high rubber boots, pick up a shovel and an empty can in the tool shed, and then go off and dig up a canful of fat worms in the well-manured far corner of the garden. Then I'll go back to the tool shed and get a fishing rod and a stout line, and a bright float, and a sharp hook, and then I'll row off into the lake, while the warm pink steam is still rising above the deep black water and the fish are waking up and hungry. I'll drop two heavy rusty anchors off the boat, and then I'll start waiting for bream and roach, and pike, and perch, and ruff to come along, until Grandmother comes out on the shore and starts shouting: "Hey! Enough already! Get back! Breakfast is ready!" and I'll shout back to her: "Tsh-sh! Don't shout! Don't scare the fish!" And it'll be like almost twenty years ago, in 1966, when my parents first discovered and then bought this place from a couple of rural septuagenarians, Dmitrii Konstantinovich and Anna Alexeyevna.

What was their last name? I couldn't remember.

That was almost a lifetime ago.

Back then, in 1966, this place was a small piece of land with only a tall old wooden house, a tool shed, a boat, a dozen apple trees, the lake, the landscape, the serenity, the silence, and the woods full of mushrooms and border guards. There had been the early mornings in the boat on the lake with Dmitrii Konstantinovich. I could, it seemed, remember every one of those ninety-six fish that I'd caught in the summer of 1966, the year of the World Soccer Cup in London on TV at our next-door neighbors'.

Not much had changed in K. since then.

And yet, although the lake appeared the same as in 1966, it wasn't. Some bio-research institute had dumped tons of experimental chemicals in the water, supposedly to weed out the small, useless, and unprofitable fish. They had proven nothing, of course, and were subsequently indicted on charges of criminal adventurism. I doubted, however, that they ever did time in jail.

Almost all the fish in the lake, big and small, had died then, and even though the survivors had turned out to be resilient—they still multiplied—fishing had never been as good since. And tomorrow would never be like twenty years ago.

That was a sad thought.

I sat on the Leo Tolstoy bench under the lime, yawning, feeling my impatience grow. I looked at my watch and got up.

I walked over to the shore and stepped into the boat, cautiously. It creaked and started rocking. I stepped out again and opened the padlock on the bow anchor line, which was wrapped around the lime trunk. Then I walked all the way down to the tool shed and picked up the oars. Back at the boat, I put them into the oarlocks and slowly pulled out.

Heavy drops of water on my oars, water's strong resistance. That I could move, weightless, over the water, never ceased to amaze me.

Soon I was in the middle of the lake, resting on my oars, looking idly around.

Now, with the sun at high noon, all the fishermen were gone from the lake. I was alone.

The lake was big, a mile wide, ten miles long, twenty-five meters deep—a rapid succession of promontories, jutting out into the water. No flies or mosquitoes could reach my boat out there. I felt the day growing hot on my skin.

I could see far across the lake. The lake's horizons were flat.

The sky was clear.

There used to be a grim-looking, sinisterly ethereal medieval cathedral, a silhouette protruding against the sky, on the far right bank of the lake. Part of an old Finnish Lutheran church, long since abandoned by the dead parishioners, it was called *kirkha*, a strange, strained word to a Russian ear. The sound of it was like a rusted pick crumbling bricks.

It had been a hallmark of our lake.

Back in 1966, it represented the end of the lake world on the outskirts of my imagination.

"The sky's so clear today, even the *kirkha* somehow

seems closer!" my grandmother would say.

I was an eleven year old. My imagination was always working overtime. I'd read many books about ghosts and nightly lonely Gothic groans and howls.

I liked that dark, exotic, medieval word: *kirkha*.

One August afternoon, when everyone—my parents, my younger brother, my grandmother—was either dozing off or drinking tea with strawberry jam on the veranda, I slipped away, unnoticed, from the sleepy conversation and the sounds of snoring, and set out on a trip to the *kirkha*, that tiny hairpin in the sky.

I rowed and rowed, unstoppably, until my arms became as hard as my oars. Finally, three hours later, I was there.

The bottom of the boat hit the silt and sand of a grisly lagoon. I sat up and held my breath in awe. The *kirkha* was immense. It had been completely burnt out inside and was the color of coagulated blood. After a moment's hesitation, I stepped out of the boat onto the marshy ground covered with split gravestones.

I looked around me.

Shriveled cigarette butts and insipid condoms, oozing some revolting milky substance, were strewn over the wet moss. Shreds of newsprint rustled under my feet. I could see huge birds and flocks of bats in the sky.

A few dozen meters away, sprawled on a giant dirty towel, a man and a woman were making love. She seemed thin; he was pretty fat. Oblivious to everything, they couldn't see me.

The sight of two tightly embraced naked bodies immediately petrified and thrilled me. My heart raced.

"So *this* is what it looks like!" I thought.

For a moment I was afraid I might faint. I made a step forward, craning my neck.

Then I realized that no one would know where to look for me if I were sucked in by the *kirkha* marshes. A flapping of leathery wings overhead filled my soul with fear.

I turned around to leave and stumbled on an over-grown stone that bore etched black lettering under the cover of dried mud. "Reiner W. Stoltz, 1420–1467," I read. The name seemed German.

And yet, the inscription had been made in Russian!

There was something fishy about this place.

I jumped back in the boat and pulled away. Soon the *kirkha* turned back into a familiar, menacingly meaning-less gray vertical line on the horizon.

Now, nineteen years later, the *kirkha* was no longer there. They'd torn it down in the mid-seventies and built in its place a correctional summer camp for juvenile delin-quents. Torn down, too, was the local milk plant. They used to dump streams of whey in the lake there. The water near its shore had always been pale and crawling with bream.

I took my hands off the oars and looked around me. A lonely hawk was circling the tall sky that was full of glar-ing sun.

I couldn't understand what I was doing here, in the middle of the lake. Rocked by the boat's cradle, I fell asleep.

In my dream, I was what I was in real life: a young man who was getting older, pushing thirty, getting on his own nerves, constantly repeating himself.

Getting older and beginning to realize that he was going to die some day.

It was actually a pleasant dream.

An army border guard helicopter over the lake awoke me. Before I knew it, its cold damp elongated shadow was all over me. The lake shuddered convulsively. I panicked. The boat began thrashing about on its two anchor chains. I fell on the bottom of the boat, covering my head with my arms.

After a while, I managed to sit back up and pull up the anchors. The helicopter stood overhead, roaring. The pilot tilted it slightly, opened the door and leaned out of his cockpit, shaking his fist.

I turned the boat around and headed for the shore.

That evening, I fell asleep at the dinner table. It was embarrassing. My grandmother and I were eating and discussing Yulian Semyonov's new KGB thriller that my grandmother had checked out of the local library. "It's so *good!*" she said. "It makes your skin *crawl!*" She told me, as if in an apology, that, had she known that I was coming, she would've gotten some fresh fish from the local poachers.

I was telling her that the chicken was superb.

It was. I was amazed by its rich taste. It was no "blue bird" from a city food store. My grandmother bought her chicken directly from the state-owned farm.

That was against the law, of course.

Then I fell asleep.

My grandmother tapped me on the shoulder: "Wake up!"

I awoke, smiled at her, and fell asleep again. I dreamed I'd won a hundred thousand rubles in Sportloto and gotten completely drunk with my friends.

I awoke again, disturbed by another dream—this time on the second floor, in the attic hayloft, on the flowery bedspread over the hay mattress, in the night, in sweat, in total darkness, on the verge of a happy breakthrough. The article about an obscure Moscow underground poet that I'd intended to start for quite a while began to take shape in my mind.

I got up from the mattress, groped my way over to the desk, and lit the desk lamp. It was very bright.

The desk was older than the house, and the lamp must have been as old as the desk.

A stack of *Ogonyok* magazines, all twelve garish issues from 1956, was sitting on the desk. I leafed through some of them, mindlessly, for a hundredth time: long solved crosswords, large pictures of Khrushchev and Chairman Mao, Nehru and Nasser, angry denunciations of Adenauer and Eisenhower, reports on the triumphs of Soviet athletes in the Melbourne Olympics and on the failed imperialist attack on socialism in Hungary; self-righteous journalism, indignant letters to the editor, rural fashion trends, last-minute weather updates, stories about recovering alcoholics and kinless cosmopolites. Also on the desk was Sabunayev's green book on fishing, published in 1956.

1956 had been good to the former owners of the house.

I peered through the night. The air was thick with the aroma of Grandmother's flowers. Up here, in the open window, ninety-six kilometers from Leningrad, the night was quiet and serene, as it never was in the city. And yet, there was a mild uneasiness in the stillness. Something big and tense, not quite dormant, was rolling over, breathing, sighing, groaning in the night. I knew I was probably imagining things. Everyone was already asleep in K.

Except for the border guards, of course. They never slept.

I closed my eyes and imagined my whole country, vast and very dark in the night, bright and sprightly—and still vast—in the morning, standing silently behind my back, ready to defend its borderless frontiers. . . . I felt a spasm of feverish delight. My country! It never slept! The sun never set on my country! It was the greatest country on the face of the Earth!

My country wasn't ever going to leave me alone.

I opened my eyes.

Across the lake, at least a kilometer away, I could see a yellow speck of light in the distance.

I was not alone, after all.

I imagined the hikers in their weatherproof jackets,

sitting by tents around the bonfire on the other side, looking intently at the flames and at the guitarist, singing in
sad, slow voices their songs about the road that never ends.
I could smell the ubiquitous potato baking in the red-hot
rubble of coals. I could see young boys and girls staring at
the flames relaxed, tired. . . .

Hiking never was encouraged in these parts, especially
on the opposite, unpopulated side of the lake, bordering on
the forbidden zone. The border guards had always viewed
the bonfires with grave suspicion.

Those hikers would be better off someplace else.

Then again, maybe I was still too full of fears.

I opened my notebook and wrote down the first sentence of my article. It came out pretty long. Then I heard
two muffled, low voices coming from behind the front gate.

I put down the pencil and held my breath. I heard low
voices again. I tiptoed over to the front attic window and
saw below two flickering cigarette tips, levitating in the
dark outside the front gate. Two smokers. One of them was
tall, the other short. They couldn't be seen in the dark, only
guessed at by the darker quality of darkness behind their
cigarettes. My heart started beating. I knew they'd tracked
me down.

One tall, another short. I wasn't nonexisting enough
for them to be happy. They'll wake up Grandmother. I could
hear her loud snoring downstairs. There was no getting away
from them.

What did they want from me?

I could stay in the attic and hope they'd be gone by
morning, but I knew I'd eventually have to go out to them.

The front door hinges needed oiling. When I walked
out of the house, surrounded by clouds of mosquitoes, the
two, still invisible, dropped their cigarettes.

"Who are you? What are you doing here?" I asked in a
firm whisper, to let them know I was not afraid of them.

There was no response.

I opened the gate.

The two moved. Now I could see them: one tall and blond, the other short and naked from the waist up. A voluminous bag was at the tall one's feet on the road. They looked like two locals.

I realized that they hadn't come here looking for me.

"What's up, guys?" I asked, instantly enormously relieved. They looked at me, smiling shyly.

"You must be G.N.'s grandson!" said the short one. "You must be Litovtsev, right?"

I nodded.

"How's the weather in Leningrad?" asked the tall guy. He was my age. He lit another cigarette.

"Sorry to've bothered you so late," the short guy said. "We just thought maybe G.N. wasn't sleeping yet." He glanced up at me with hope: "Is she?"

"Guys, it's almost twelve-thirty," I said.

"We're sorry," said the tall guy, shifting from one foot to another. "We just thought, maybe she wanted some fresh fish . . ."

"What fish, guys? It's almost half past twelve!" I said.

"Zander," the short guy breathed out timidly.

"A nice fresh little sucker!" the tall guy said, vigorously nodding his head.

"Almost three kilos! A giant!" the short guy said proudly.

"She always tells us she prefers zander over maybe perch or pike," the tall guy said.

"We have pike and perch too!" the short guy added hastily. "They're *nice!*" He pointed to the bag.

I looked at them, smiling. The only way to catch a zander in the lake was to net it, and netting fish in the lake was against the law, but so was selling fish.

The tall guy looked at me, grinning. "Don't tell anybody in Leningrad," he said.

"It's all right," I said. "I'm a friend."

I almost loved them at this moment.

These two guys, I thought, the local poachers—they could've roughed me up, they could've gotten mad at me for one reason or another, they could've been someplace else now, drinking vodka and talking, or sleeping with their women. But instead they were here, in the night, in front of our house, smiling, smoking, slightly drunk, anxious to sell their fish to me. I felt growing warmth in my chest.

"How much?" I asked.

They exchanged swift glances. Their eyes started gleaming.

"A bottle," said the tall one quickly. His Adam's apple bobbed. It wasn't a statement, it was a question, a shy request.

I imagined an ice-cold green-glass bottle of Andropovka glistening with icy sweat, its terrible taste on my tongue.

"One tiny little bottle of vodka!" the short one said dreamily. The tall guy gave him a nudge with his elbow.

"I don't know where my grandmother hides the bottles," I said, ruefully. "I'm really sorry. I could give you some money. . . ."

"Some money!" exclaimed the tall guy. "That'd be fine! Give us some money! We can buy vodka from old Levashikha right now, and you're invited!"

For a moment I was considering going off and getting drunk with them, but then I started feeling tense and impatient again. I knew I'd ruin their night.

"Thank you, guys, but I'm afraid I shouldn't be drinking tonight," I said. "Look, I got seven rubles on me. . . ."

"That's just fine!" said the short one hastily. "Seven's Levashikha's bottom line, that's a great coincidence!" He began to open the bag.

I suspected that Levashikha's bottom line was six or

five, but it didn't matter. I had seven ruble bills left after having paid for my early breakfast in Zyelenogorsk with a ten.

I handed them the money.

They staggered off into the night. The zander was wrapped in a local newspaper. It was fresh. I weighed it in my hands. It was heavy. It did, indeed, weigh at least three kilos.

A good buy, I thought. A good bargain. A good zander. Good guys. A good day, all in all. I sneaked back in the house and put the fish in the refrigerator. I imagined my grandmother's eyes when she found it there. She'd be pleased. She'd know that I wanted her to be pleased.

Good grandson! she'd think.

I climbed up the squeaky stairs, noiselessly. The light was yellow and cozy in the attic.

I sat again at the desk, watching the yellow light's bright circle on the green paper. The hikers were still sitting around their bonfire across the lake. I started writing again.

Then I heard a scratching sound overhead. I glanced up and saw a small bat, half the length of my palm, hanging head down from a tiny crack between the roof beams right above the window frame. It looked like a toy black umbrella. "Hi, there!" I said, startled. I had never seen a bat so close before.

Its eyes were closed

I stared for some time at its miniature dog's snub-nosed square face.

The bat was sleeping. It seemed weightless. It was velvety, the same fabric as in those Russian rural women's jackets of the early thirties.

"Wake up!" I said. "I want to see your eyes!"

The bat twitched its ear.

"Dumb, dumb bat!" I said. It occurred to me that I probably sounded like an idiot.

But then, I was alone up here!

I knew that bats were almost blind but could somehow distinguish between light and darkness. They fell asleep at sunrise, like Count Dracula. The bat must have been deceived by the lamp light in the attic and decided that it was daytime, bedtime.

I pressed the switch button and immersed the attic in night.

Then I turned the light back on. The bat was asleep.

I pushed the button on and off, merging light with darkness, at the rate of a mad heartbeat, until my eyes could no longer stand it. I stopped, leaving the light on.

The bat was still sleeping. Then it yawned, just like a dog—or a man—revealing the sudden pinkness of its mouth. I was deeply moved.

"Oh, you!" I said. "You feel comfortable up here, with me, don't you? You know I'm a friend, don't you?"

I felt like touching it with my fingers.

It crossed my mind that I was probably the only man on Earth at this moment who was sitting at a desk by a window watching a bat sleeping in his attic room.

I was probably one of the very few people on Earth who'd ever seen a sleeping bat yawn!

I went back to my writing.

I realized that something was disturbing my eyes. I looked at the other side of the lake and saw a light flashing in a codelike manner. It was not the hikers' fire: something else was illuminating the night.

It was very strong.

It didn't take me long to realize what was going on: the hikers had, no doubt, noticed the lonely second-floor window on the other side of the lake run amok, and decided that a desperate insomniac was sending forth some kind of lonely message to the world. Now they were responding to that message by using a high-powered flashlight.

Their flashlight was strong enough to be seen every-where and by everyone who was still awake.

Someone was letting me know, in a codelike pattern, that I was not alone.

But I already knew that.

"Hey, bat!" I said loudly, recalling that bats have incredibly acute hearing: they can hear ultrasonic sounds.

The bat was sleeping. My voice wasn't high-pitched enough for its ears.

I scratched the desktop with my fingernail and cringed: I didn't like the sound.

The bat still didn't awaken.

Then another sound, a whole army of sounds, began rocking the land, the house, and the water: the helicopters again. They were closing in on the lake and our house, and for a moment I thought a war had just begun. In a minute everything was shrieking and vibrating with terror.

The light in my grandmother's room went on. The roof started singing. The lights went on along the string of scat-tered houses on our side of the lake. The helicopters, four or five of them, illuminated from within, proceeded through the sky across the lake, crumpling the water, bending the treetops, horrifying the fish, deafening the beasts in the woods. Across the lake, they hovered over the hikers' bon-fire. Then they disappeared in the night, and soon every-thing was dark and quiet again.

Silence was a thin, shrill needlepoint in the skull. Without opening my eyes, I knew that the lights on our side of the lake had gone off. My grandmother turned off the light in her room. I opened my eyes, looking at the desktop.

I wished I hadn't come here.

When I looked out again, the other side of the lake was dark. For a moment I thought I could discern the night's darker shade of darkness where the recent fire had been laid, as if the light, extinguished, had left an enormously black, cold coal in its place.

Then the darkness of the night evened out.

I wouldn't have been surprised, looking up, to find that the bat had been swept away by the helicopters' raging waves of air, but it was still there, sleeping. The night was warm and clear. I saw what no one else could see: the light from my window had made a long beam of light, like a seesaw plank extending over the lake. The lower end of the beam was buried under the dark coals on the other side.

I realized that maybe the border guards, too, could see what I saw, and reached out to close my window.

My elbow knocked a stack of magazines off the desk. The house shuddered with their weight. Now I only could see my face in the mirror of the window.

Downstairs, I heard my grandmother's angry coughing. "Are you out of your mind?" she asked me loudly from her room. "What are you doing up there—teasing the border guards? Do you know what time it is?"

I turned off the light.

Bologoye

My best friend is afraid of his father-in-law. "I still love my wife," he sighs, "but I don't think I can stand her crazy father much longer!"

"That's a shame," I say, pausing in front of the newsstand. *Pravda, Leningradskaya Pravda, Izvestiya.*

He pulls at my sleeve. "Come on, you've already read those! Tell me: what should I do? I respect my wife, but her father hates me!"

I laugh. He frowns: "What's so funny?"

"Gorbachev has made the front page of *Pravda*!"

He pouts. "You're not listening! I'm talking about my *family life*! Maybe I should divorce my wife! Her father is dangerous!"

"Everyone is dangerous," I point out.

"That's true," he says. "But I don't have to share an apartment with everyone. Besides, not everyone is an unpredictable nut."

"Everyone, everyone is a nut," I say, feeling smug.

"That's true," he says. "But I'm not afraid of other nuts. They can't hurt me. Other nuts at least age gracefully. They don't scream 'Get out!' when I walk into their room hoping to watch some TV."

"Don't walk into his room," I suggest.

"I don't!" he says. "I try to stay away from him as much as I can!"

"You're exaggerating," I say. We walk on in silence.

We are two young men in a crowd. It's Saturday, the best time of the week. Fresh from the weekly downtown bathhouse, we walk along Liteiny Prospekt, past the beer bar and KGB headquarters, to the Kolkhoz Market. We feel good. One of our bathhouse friends is throwing a party nearby and we have to buy a hunk of lamb. Vodka has been getting harder to find since they started closing down the liquor stores late last May, but our bathhouse friend's relative works in a big restaurant and can always sell us a dozen bottles from his home stock. Now, as we approach the market, the bottles are already rolling lazily in the bathtub under streams of cold tap water. The very thought of them makes me thirsty.

"Tell your father-in-law to be patient," I suggest. "Talk to him. Be kind. Let him know that you care. He's afraid of dying, that's all. Tell him that soon scientists will reprogram his genetic code and he won't have to die. Tell him to quit smoking and drinking and wait."

"He doesn't drink, he doesn't smoke," my best friend says.

"Threaten him. Tell him that you're going to write a letter to his Party Committee."

"He's not a member of the Party."

"You must be exaggerating," I say.

It's fall, but it feels like spring. A minute ago clouds were all over the Leningrad sky; now the sky is clean blue.

We buy two glasses of diluted beer from the market beer-stand.

"What lousy beer!" he says, blowing off the heavy foam.

I agree: "The worst."

He smiles contentedly. "But at least we can afford it! Yesterday I was buying beer near my house. There was a line. A bum with no money was begging for a glass of beer. He kept saying: 'I'm not asking you for a fancy car or a marble palace with fountains, just buy me a glass of beer!' I bought him a glass of beer. He said: 'You've just made me the happiest man alive!' Two hours later, when I came downstairs for another glass, he walked up to me again. 'I'm not asking you for a glass of vodka, just buy me a glass of beer!' he said. So I bought him a glass of beer, to see if he would recognize me. 'You've just made me the happiest man alive!' he said. People are so miserable!" He shakes his head, savoring his beer.

"See that man in the pink overcoat? He's been listening to us!" I say loudly. The man in dirty pink glances at me, peels himself off the beerstand, and walks away. He's drunk. We look at each other, smiling.

I leave the party on Sunday night and get into a cab. Thinking I'm too drunk to notice, the driver intends to take me home along the right bank of the Neva—a five-ruble trick. "I'm watching you!" I tell him. He shrugs. I stumble and stagger my way upstairs. "I stumble, but I rarely fall," as my girlfriend often says—usually out of context. Two flights of stairs, three, four, five. Now I'm home.

Late next morning, hungover, I gulp down a teapot of stale water and cautiously open my door. I hear hurried steps

downstairs. They become inaudible and are followed by the
sigh and shudder of the front door as someone bursts out.
None of today's newspapers are left on the newsstand
downstairs—no *Pravda*, no *Leningradskaya Pravda*, no
Izvestiya: only old magazines. I go back up through the dark
doorway to the two-tiered set of plywood mailboxes along
the green wall. I pause, looking around, holding my breath
before dipping my fingers through the wide crack between
the upper plank and the rough edge of the front casing,
deep into the innards of someone's mailbox. There are several accessible boxes I can choose from, but most of them
don't interest me. I know which box has a copy of *Pravda*,
and two others—*Izvestiya* and *Leningradskaya Pravda*. I have
to act quickly, but the heartwarming feeling of discovering
the thin sheet under my fingertips makes me linger, as
always, enjoying the danger—more imaginary than real,
yet still sweet.

Back up in my room, I sit at the table, preparing to
read. Every time I open a newspaper, a part of me hopes
for something extraordinary to have happened overnight,
as if the paper would, indeed, print something truly
extraordinary; something extraordinarily true. I close my
eyes, I hold my breath, knowing that in a moment, when I
take a glance at the headlines, the suspense will be gone
and the hope—pleasantly naive, ridiculous—will vanish: the
borders will not be proclaimed open; the KGB will not have
been disbanded; who am I fooling? I might just as well take
a nap. Still, I'm sitting in my chair, waiting. It's nice to be
alone.

Every time I read a newspaper, recognizing by experience the real meaning of each word that has been omitted,
I feel sad, and even a little scared: so much has happened
in the world overnight! Indeed, while I was asleep, people
were born and killed, speeches were delivered, men and
women fell in love and made love. . . . All while I was asleep.

I fold the newspapers.

I hear steps behind my door. I sit up. It could be the super with a subpoena from the district commandant's office, or a voluntary people's militia patrol checking their list of politically unreliable locals. I'm not home. All my friends know that I never open the door without first having been contacted by phone. All my *close* friends know the secret code of ringing my doorbell: two short rings, one long, one short. I'm nobody's fool. I wait, but nothing happens and I begin to dial the number of a friend of mine who works at the Moskovsky train station ticket office. My best friend and I are going to Moscow tomorrow, for a day—to get away from Leningrad. I keep getting busy signals, then she picks up the phone. "A tough order on such short notice, honey," she says, in a sweet voice. I promise her a box of chocolates, a bottle of champagne, and seven rubles. "Seven? Why seven? Why not six or eight?" she asks, intrigued. We agree on ten.

I open my door and, a box of chocolates in my bag, leave to pick up the tickets. Champagne shouldn't be a problem: Leningrad alcoholics don't drink champagne; it's expensive. They respect it too much. They don't appreciate the idea of bubbles.

When I get back home five hours later, there's the word "Scum" scribbled on my door with white chalk. I look around, ready to bolt. I hold my breath. I wipe the chalk off with my sleeve.

I go downstairs, to the fourth floor, and find the same inscription on one of the doors there. I go upstairs, to the sixth floor: all the doors are clean. I go all the way down, to the first floor, and find one of the doors there also marked by some miserable nut. These things happen. I return to my room.

Whenever I walk in from outside, my room always makes my heart leap with joy. It's dusty, it's a mess, but it's mine. When I come in from outside and latch and lock the door, looking at the books on the shelves, the pictures on the walls, the papers and the typewriter on the table, the empty bottles in the corner, a porcelain figurine of a ballerina on top of the old TV, I feel that I have finally arrived. I feel safe and strong. A moment before I was outside, in the open, and now I'm in here, unhurried. When the phone starts to ring, I can pick it up if I want to, or I can read a paper instead.

The phone rings. I do pick it up and say in a changed, low voice, as I always do when I am not sure who is calling (which I never am): "Speaking."

It's my mother. She sounds urgent: "I need to see you."

"Do you want me to come over?" I say. She lives five blocks down the street.

"No. We'll meet outside."

"Mother, it's cold and dark outside!"

"So?" she says. "So what? Are you suddenly afraid of the dark?"

"So do you want to come over?" I say.

She sighs impatiently: "Don't be stupid. It's important. We can't talk about it now, don't you understand?"

Instantly concerned, I laugh good-naturedly: "Oh mother, you don't seriously believe that both our places are—"

"Shut up!" she exclaims, frightened.

"All right, all right! If you don't want me to say that you believe that both our places are bugged, I won't! I'll meet you in five minutes." We hang up.

I meet her in ten minutes; she is close to tears. Late last night someone called her on the phone and told her that her son had just been run over by a truck. She dropped the phone on the floor. When she picked it back up, the caller laughed and said that he was only joking. However, he added, today's joke is often tomorrow's reality. "What do you want from me?" she asked. "Nothing. I'm a friend and I would hate to see you upset," he said, hanging up.

I'm scared. A wave of helpless anger washes all over me. I smile bravely, confidently, and hug her: "Mother, the world is full of nasty people! That was just a crank call. He didn't even know your name, or mine. Believe me, it's not worth your tears!"

"I don't believe you," she says, dabbing her eyes with a handkerchief. "I want to, but I can't. They're after you, can't you see? I don't know why, but they are!"

"Let's go up to my place and get drunk!" I suggest. Whenever I'm with her, I feel wise and strong—simply because she's not.

"Promise me you'll stop doing whatever they want you to stop doing!" she says.

"Give me some more time!" I ask her. "Things are changing everywhere."

"No they are not!" she says.

"Not yet," I admit.

"I'm scared, I'm scared!" she says.

I want to say: So am I! So am I!

I say: "I have some good French wine up in my room!"

"You're lying," she says, smiling through the tears.

"I'm not!" I lie angrily.

"Stop being an alcoholic! Please!" she screams suddenly. Compared to her, everyone is an alcoholic.

"Mother, you're overreacting," I say.

Late at night, after the late news on TV, I go to bed, leaving the flickering TV and the lights on; that way I feel more secure, as if I were not alone in the room. I don't like falling asleep. I just like waking up in the morning. If for some reason I don't wake up, the lights in my room, seen from the street, will let whoever might be worried by my non-existence—my mother, my best friend, my girlfriend—know that something is wrong. I just can't picture myself as a corpse. My worst fear is *not* that I'm going to die in my sleep, but that no one would know I was dead. For a moment I'm filled with self-pity. Then I imagine what I must look like now: a grown man, old enough to be someone's father, lying in bed with the lights on, healthy, and thinking about being dead. I start to laugh cautiously, silently. Then I imagine myself lying in bed and laughing at the picture of myself lying in bed and laughing, and I start to laugh louder. My neighbor to the left bangs his fist against the wall: "Young man! Let me sleep! Do you know what time it is?" He never protests when I have a noisy bunch of friends over late at night. I can't remember what he looks like. His irritated, reassuring voice makes me wonder how I could have possibly felt forgotten and forlorn a moment ago. It reminds me of an old joke—two men are drinking wine late at night; one man asks the other, in whose room they're drinking, "What's that huge piece of wood doing on your bed?"

"That's my late-night clock," the other man says.

"How so?"

"Watch this." He grabs it and brings it hard against the wall. Immediately comes the neighbor's muffled groan: "For Christ's sake! Are you out of your mind? It's two-thirty in the morning!"

I laugh again, this time very loudly. My neighbor slams the wall with his fist.

Next morning I decide against going downstairs for the newspapers. Instead, I leaf through some old magazines, waiting. Soon I hear steps outside. I tiptoe to the door and

hold my breath. There are *steps* outside my door! I press
my eye against the keyhole. I can see the midsection of a
man cautiously moving around outside. He doesn't know
that I'm just a few steps away, watching him. If he starts
writing on my door, I'll unlock it, quickly, silently, and throw
it open. "Ouch!" I'll say. "Sorry, comrade, I didn't know
you were there! I didn't mean to smash your face in!" He'll
slouch against the elevator door, and swaying like a Hasid
in prayer, he'll cover his face and moan. "Comrade, did I
hurt you?" I'll exclaim, rushing to him. "Did I break your
nose? Let me see! It's okay, it's happened to me!"

It has. Once, when I was in high school, three friends
of mine were waiting for me outside, unaware that I had a
habit of pressing my forehead against the door when I was
tired before pushing it open. They knew that it was me
coming out, but they didn't know that it was my *face* they
were hitting when they jokingly kicked the door back shut
with their feet. I broke my nose then; I fell like a sack of
flour. Then, still unconscious, I jumped to my feet and
sprinted off. My friends, scared out of their minds, caught
up with me, grabbed my hands, and led me away from the
marshy wasteland surrounding the school building to my
grandmother's. She wasn't home. I came to and saw my
face in the mirror.

"You were saying things when we dragged you to your
grandmother's!" my friends told me later.

"I was unconscious!" I pointed out to them.

"You kept saying: 'Oh God, a minute ago everything
was fine! Oh God, a minute ago everything was good!' "

"Really? I think you're exaggerating," I said.

I hear the man's footsteps move to the neighbor's door.
Silence, and then the sound of chalk against dry wood. Then
the man turns around and hurries down the stairs. I open
my door and follow him. Once in the street, I look around,
and since it's daytime and the street is empty, I can see his

back. He's middle-aged and shorter than me. He still doesn't know that I'm watching him. He drops into the doorway across the court. I wait outside.

After some time, he walks back out, and glances around. I'm hidden behind the kindergarten fence; he can't see me. He walks off; I follow. He's in my power now.

I follow him for fifteen minutes as he methodically steps into every second doorway along his route. Then I grow impatient and decide to confront him. He's older, smaller, weaker than me. Maybe I won't even hit him; maybe I'll just slap him on the shoulder from behind: "Hi, scum!" Then suddenly his walk changes: it becomes leisurely. He deviates from the pattern of doorways, takes off his hat and smooths his skimpy hair. He is now a tired working man headed home. I wait until he disappears in his doorway, two blocks away from mine, and then follow him inside. I hear a door up on the third floor slam shut. I'm good at locating the sources of sounds, and when I'm on the third floor, I know which door is his. I pull a piece of paper and a pencil out of my pocket. Leaning against his door, I write: "I'll be watching your every step!" I leave the note on his doormat and go back to my room.

I want to take a shower before the trip to Moscow, but there's no water in the hissing rusty bathroom pipes. These things happen. I pack my bag, get into a cab, and go to my girlfriend's place. She's not home. I take a shower, then she returns from work, we make love, and I take a shower again and leave for the Moskovsky train station.

There are four clear days ahead of me—a day in Moscow, three days in Leningrad. Once a week I am a night-guard at a public park on the outskirts of Leningrad, and my next shift is on Sunday. I'm supposed to be there every other night, but my boss doesn't mind my being absent for a week: partly because I pay him ten rubles from my

monthly salary—eighty rubles, which can buy twelve bottles of cheap vodka, or could, when vodka was easy to find—
and also because a public park doesn't need to be guarded
at night anyway.

My best friend and I meet five minutes before the
departure. We love trains. We've spent years on the railroad. Late at night, when you're both tired and alert, no
one and nothing depends on you, nothing is expected of
you, except accepting the roadbed, which unfolds over dark
terrain. You wake up to a rusty plateau under the rain
and three trees. You wake up the next morning to see the
same. You can travel for days without ever seeing anything else. Water is boiling on the stove, the coals smell
like hot iron, the conductor is drunk, three unshaven
men in your compartment are sipping wine and playing cards while you're reading a slow novel on the upper
bunk and thinking pleasant and instantly forgettable
thoughts.

The train leaves at midnight to a brass-band rendition
of "The Great City's Hymn" on the station radio. It's a Red
Arrow train, plush and comfortable, a Soviet version of the
Orient Express.

There are two other passengers in our compartment,
and we can't drink, although we bought some wine for the
trip. Drinking has been strictly prohibited on the railroad
ever since they started their anti-alcohol campaign late last
May. All we can do is talk.

And so we talk. We look out the window and see the
succession of dark hills nearby and strings of bright
unblinking lights in the distance. We walk out of our compartment to the only place where we can't be found, at least
for a while—the rocking space between two cars. We quickly
down two bottles of wine. Soon the other two passengers
go to bed, falling asleep in the blue shade of overhead lamps,

and we finish the rest of our wine. Halfway through the journey, the train makes a stop in Bologoye. It's a tiny town in the middle of nowhere. Moscow is three and a half hours away. Leningrad is three and a half hours away. It's a dark place, too, at two-thirty in the morning. Its name makes no sense: Bologoye. It's as if whoever settled down here first just mumbled something under his breath in frustration, and then he thought: "Hey, that's what I'm going to call this dump from now on: Bologoye!"

"It's hard to believe people may actually live here," my friend says, gazing out the window. I remember my first trips to Moscow, when I was five or six and used to spend as much time in Moscow as in Leningrad. My grandmother lived most of her life in Moscow, but her daughter—my mother—lived in Leningrad, and Grandmother had to make a choice between the two cities. Whenever she went back to Moscow for a visit, which happened once every three months, she would take me along. Each time I was genuinely surprised that people could fall asleep on the train, as if they weren't going to Moscow and that night was no different from any other night. My grandmother would fall asleep, too. One night I slipped out of the compartment into the empty corridor. Halfway through the trip, the train made a stop in Bologoye. I looked at the building behind the station office. High above, in the only illuminated window, was a bearded man in a white shirt. He was looking out and seemed young and pensive. I liked the idea of he and I being the only two nonsleepers in the world. It occurred to me that I would never see him again. I waved to him, but he didn't see me. I was just about to get off the train, while my grandmother was still asleep, when the train pulled out.

"Show me that building," my best friend says, after I tell him the story.

"I haven't been able to find it since," I say guiltily. "But I'm sure it was there."

"If you had actually gotten off that train, it would've made a good story," he says.

We discuss the trains for a while. Then we fall asleep. Three and a half hours later we are in Moscow; thirty hours later we are back in Leningrad.

I take a cab home from the train station. When I approach my doorway, two old women, who always sit on the bench by the outer wall of the building, nod and giggle. One of them says: "Young man!"

I stop: "What's up, ladies?"

"No, nothing!" they say, still giggling.

"What's that, citizens?"

"No, nothing!" they say.

There are wet spots on the steps by the elevator, and a note on my doormat: "You've flooded our apartments, you irresponsible man!"

The floor in my room is soaking wet. Water stands in lakes on the tiled floor in the bathroom. I try the shower: no water in the pipes, but the shower handle is turned on. I realize what's happened: when I discovered that there was no water before I left for Moscow, I hurried to my girlfriend's, forgetting that I had left the shower handle turned on. Later that night, water must have started pouring into the tub.

I rush downstairs, to the fourth floor. All four flooded tenants silently step out of their doors.

I've destroyed their apartments. The ceilings have fallen down, the plaster on the walls is cracked and the chairs stand in water nearly fifty centimeters high over the carpets.

They tried to break into my place, the tenants tell me, but the door wouldn't give—I grin sheepishly, proudly: "Of course not!"—and they called the superintendent's office instead. There was much fuss. They cut the water supply off, but it was too late. I keep nodding mournfully, until my neck starts to ache.

Strangely enough, the worst damage has been done to the third-floor apartment, not the one on the fourth floor. The third-floor tenant, an old, frail woman, shows me a heavy piece of ceiling that nearly killed her in her sleep. "It landed on my pillow next to my *face!*" she says.

I weigh it in my hand: it's heavy. The thought that I might have been an unknowing murderer while sitting in a train to Moscow, makes me shiver. "It almost *killed* me!" she repeats, as if unable to comprehend the idea of being dead.

"Oh, you're exaggerating," I say.

An hour later the four tenants and I are sitting around the table in my room. They intend to sue me. I suggest a more pragmatic approach. I have a friend who can repaint their apartments for a small fee, and I'm willing to pay the damages. But if we get the court officials involved, I say, it will take the four of them years before they see my money.

"Obviously, you're not planning on being around here for years," the second-floor tenant observes ironically. He's an old bald man.

"What do you mean?" I ask. I know what he means.

He purses his lips. "Obviously, someone in this room is planning on leaving this country soon. Forever. Am I wrong?" He is right, of course. But how did he know?

There is a pause. "That's none of your business!" I say. I'm supposed to look indignant.

He shakes his head. "Look, I've been a member of the

Party since 1938, a veteran of the War, and let me tell you: back in those days, we knew how to treat a traitor!" There's another awkward pause in the room. Poor old jerk!

"Your life is almost over, and you're so angry!" I say. He glares at me.

"So it's you we have to be thankful to now that we're up the creek without a paddle, comrade revolutionary?" says a first-floor tenant, a middle-aged woman in thick glasses. "Look what you've done to this country!"

The old man waves hopelessly.

"Three hundred rubles," I say. "Total."

They start arguing. Everyone claims that his apartment has suffered greater damage. "Five hundred!" the old man says.

"You shouldn't be thinking about money!" a fourth-floor tenant points out to him. "You should be thinking about the world revolution, you old idiot!"

"That is neither here nor there," I say.

"Five hundred!" he repeats adamantly. We agree on four.

I have no idea where to get four hundred rubles. I'll have to stop eating. I'll have to stop drinking. I'll have to stop riding around in cabs.

I'll have to sell most of my books.

I start mopping up the floor. I had been meaning to have it washed for years; now it just doesn't need washing. That's good. I pick up a dozen books from the floor. They're wet, their pages glued together. They can't be sold.

Suddenly I feel an attack of nausea; cold sweat pops out on my forehead. It's hard to breathe; I don't know what to do. I start to panic: what's wrong with me? Am I dying? What if I have some kind of cancer? I rush to the bathroom and bend over the sink, trying to throw up. My heart is pounding, my eyes go blind. In the mirror, they're bloodshot. I stagger off, thinking: "So *this* is how it happens!" I collapse on the bed and fall asleep.

I'm awakened by the ringing of the phone. Normally, I don't awaken easily. The phone rings with impatient authority.

"Is Comrade Yevgeny Litovtsev home?" asks an official female voice.

"He's not home," I say in a changed voice.

"Comrade Litovtsev, please stop fooling, will you?" the woman says with sudden chumminess.

"Who's speaking?" I ask. "Are you a friend of his? Would you like to leave a message for him?"

"You men!" she says playfully. "Comrade Litovtsev, according to my records here, we've talked fourteen times over the last several years, both on the phone and otherwise. I personally feel like I've known you forever! Do you really not know who I am?"

"I'm hanging up now!" I say, but I don't. I know who she is. I feel numb. She's never talked to me like this before.

"This is Inspector Zvereva from the District Office of Visas. Comrade Litovtsev, where have you been? I called you yesterday."

"I'm around, I'm around," I say.

"Congratulations! You've been granted an exit permit! You must leave in a month. . . . Are you there?"

"I'm here," I say.

"Congratulations! You've been granted—"

"Oh, cut it out, comrade!"

She is silent for a moment. Then her voice becomes businesslike.

"You have to come to my office early next week, with six photographs of yourself, six by nine centimeters. And remember, don't take your picture with a hat on. You will be given a list of signatures to obtain from various organizations and hospitals. Then you'll have to go to Moscow to complete the paperwork."

"Damn it, inspector, I've just returned from Moscow!" I say.

"We know," she says, hanging up.
I return to bed and fall back to sleep.

In the morning, I'm awakened by the phone. It rings every
fifteen minutes. I take a cab to my girlfriend's place. She
doesn't have a phone. No one knows I'm here. She's at work.

I sit around reading her newspapers: an earthquake in
Mexico; a tornado in the American Midwest; a strike in
France; new disarmament initiatives coming from Moscow; a housewife from Byelorussia has found a gigantic
mushroom in her garden. Then my girlfriend finally comes
home. We drink wine; I tell her that I'm leaving soon. "For
how long?" she asks. "I don't know. Probably forever," I
say, and repeat, "Yes, forever, forever. Definitely forever,"
hurting her, of course. Why? Maybe because the harsher
the words, the less attention she is going to pay to them.
She nods. Then she puts her glass down on the table and
starts shivering. I look at her; she doesn't look at me. "Stop
it!" I say. "Please." She keeps shivering. "Will you cut it
out?" She shakes her head. "Honey, you're overreacting," I
say.

We go to bed, determined to make love with the final
tenderness of imminent and irreversible separation, but our
minds are too preoccupied with that finality, and we end
up drinking more wine instead. We sit at the table, looking
outside.

I leave early in the morning. It's Saturday, bathhouse
day. I try to get a cab, but there are none in the quiet streets
of my girlfriend's neighborhood. Usually it's easier in Leningrad to get a ride from a 'privateer,' someone who owns
a private car, but Saturday mornings there aren't many of
those either, and I wave my hand in vain until, almost an
hour later, a tan Zhiguli pulls up at the curb. I climb into
the back seat and tell the driver my destination. He nods

and switches on the morning music. I look out the window.

As we approach my part of Leningrad, he glances at me in the mirror: "Leaving, Litovtsev? That's not good. Normally I don't drive traitors around in my car."

"Here we are!" I say, startled.

"My personal opinion is that you belong in jail," he says, smiling. "What do you think?"

"I didn't know you people have to work weekends!" I say.

He shrugs, as if to say: I don't mind.

We pass by the neighborhood where my family lived for years. The upper Kupchino. It wasn't until I was eighteen that we moved away. That was long before I moved into my own place.

"I don't think you have instructions to hassle me, do you?" I ask. Not that I expect him to say, You bet I do.

"Of course not. I'm just a driver," he says.

We proceed in silence. Then he turns to me: "Leaving the country of your birth, huh? I'm going to miss you. Are you going to miss me?"

I shrug. "You're too cute."

"You know what? I think you've already had all the happiness in life that you're entitled to," he says pompously. I can't keep from laughing.

"You're exaggerating," I say.

He pulls up in front of the bathhouse. I offer him three rubles. He shakes his head. I climb out of the car.

"Have a good bath!" he says.

I walk in; then I turn around, feeling uneasy. He's following me, smiling. "Are you coming too?" I ask.

"Are you coming too?" he asks.

I smile. He frowns: "What's so funny?"

"I've never seen a naked plainclothesman before!" I explain.

He sighs. "Don't be naive. Of course you have!"

My best friend and I slip out of the bathhouse an hour before
the end of the session. We keep looking back nervously, but
the man is nowhere in sight. We've shaken him off. We look
at each other, smiling.

Late at night, in my best friend's house, I knock on the door
to his father-in-law's room. I have a half-empty bottle of
vodka in my hand. My best friend tries to pull me away
from the door.

There's no answer. I walk in. His father-in-law turns
from the window. I hold out the bottle in my hand. He shakes
his head. I take a gulp.

"I have some good and some bad news for you," I say,
and extend my hand for him to shake. "The bad news is
that the sun will only continue to shine for five billion more
years; after that it will brighten for a while and then dim
and the solar system will become dark and cold, and if we
manage to survive until then, we'll still die. The good news
is that, chances are, by that time mankind will have discovered a way to do without the sun!"

He continues staring at me, probably thinking: Who
the hell is this? Then he turns back to the window.

I take another gulp; then I leave. When I reach the first
floor, I can hear sounds in the doorway: the shuffling of
invisible feet, silent voices. I open the first-floor window,
step onto the sill, and jump out. I land on my feet; then I
fall on my knees. I've injured my leg. That's unfortunate. I
turn the street corner, limping, and look back up, at the
bright second-floor window. My best friend's father-in-law
is still standing there, looking out. I grin and wave. He turns
away. My leg hurts. I stop a cab. "I don't care if you know
me!" I warn the driver.

He looks at me and yawns.

He has to take me home along the right bank of the

Neva, because it's late and all the big drawbridges are opening. I have time to think: what if I arrive at my door and find it ominously, darkly ajar? Should I walk right in? What if there's something scribbled on my door and as I'm wiping it off someone jumps me from behind?

But nothing happens. My entryway is quiet; my door is clean and locked. I fish for the keys in my pocket. I can't find them. These things happen. I must have lost my keys jumping from the window. It occurs to me that my morning driver could have stolen them from my pocket when we were in the bathhouse. That's a disconcerting thought.

There's a strip of light under my door. I sit down on the stairs. It's two-thirty in the morning. I hear the front door downstairs. Then I hear steps. I get up and thrust my shoulder against the door. It won't give. I hit it, and then I hit it again. I sit down on the stairs, exhausted. Then I get up and hit it again. It won't give. I hit it again.

People upstairs and downstairs step out of their rooms, screaming, "Let us sleep!" Finally I break in.

My heart leaps with joy. I sit at the table, reading the old newspapers, thinking about the people who have left this country before me. They were full of bitterness and anger. Suspecting their apartments would be turned over to the District Department of Visas after they left, some of them peeled off wallpaper in their living rooms and made a hole in the wall, where they'd hide a fresh egg. Then they'd cover the hole with a plaster slab and wallpaper.

I'll do no such thing. After all, I'm a reasonable man. Maybe I'll put a note under the doormat: "I'll be watching your every step!" or "I'll be back!"—it will add suspense to their lives, whoever they are—them—even though I know that I won't be back. Then again, maybe I will, in another life. It's easy to become sentimental at this hour.

Soon it starts to look like morning outside. Leaving my broken door open, I go downstairs, to the newsstand.

Insomnia

I was never good at telling intelligent people from mere self-confident fools, the know-it-alls, because I didn't and couldn't know, growing up, that, of course, those who claim to possess the whole truth usually know little or nothing. Growing up in Leningrad, the city named after a domestic god of this century, I hadn't always been taught timidity, but I couldn't help thinking that power deserves at least *some* respect.

Power, of course, was what the heavy-jawed, self-confident, laconic local officials in ill-fitting suits had in abundance: they could destroy me and everyone around me, but they could also protect me. Of course, they were supposed to be right all the time.

I knew they were thought of as fools. I also knew they were clever.

They were pawns, pitifully despicable and disposable, and yet they were strong and fearsome.

They didn't know sophisticated words.

They were bad listeners.

They spoke with the finality of omniscient illiterates.

They had sleepy eyes, half hidden behind short eyelashes and always ready to fix their cold and arrogant stare upon you unexpectedly.

Sometimes they would wink at you.

They were tiny cogs in a huge, unstoppable, menacingly rumbling machine.

They were weasels.

I used to think about them all the time. They were everywhere. I saw them on TV in black and white and, a little later, as a petty petitioner, in their oak-paneled offices, under the ubiquitous portrait of a squinting Lenin. Businesslike, they looked like parodies of themselves.

"It's *you* again!" they would say, bored. I felt angry and ashamed. My thoughts about them were unclear. They were pawns; they were my enemies; so what?

I had to keep reminding myself constantly that I hated them and didn't want to live in the same country with them.

They kept telling me I couldn't leave.

"I don't want to live in the same country with you!" I felt like shouting out proudly and meaninglessly. Of course, not once did I cross the border separating reasonable smugness from recklessness. I was no fool.

Besides, I knew what they would say, smiling, in response: "Commit suicide, Comrade Litovtsev, because you are not going anywhere!"

What I *didn't* know then was that if they had told me, "You may go. Who are we to be the judges of your life?"—I probably would have stayed.

"You can't and won't go," they persisted. Then, out of sheer frustration, I would say something witty and sardonic: "Do you know that you, too, are going to die one day?"

They would simply stare at me, coldly, coyly, condescendingly.

And then, one day, they told me I was free to go. "Really? You mean it?" They nodded gravely.

They probably forgot about me forever as soon as I left.

They were easy to despise and nice to hate, but they must have made me helpless, too: soon after I had left, I began missing the uncomplicated comfort of their belief that life can and should be beaten into submission; that death is avoidable, unlike the boss's love and wrath; and that he who is too clever—or ever in doubt—is stupid.

I thought about them as the plane took off with a roar. I was wondering about the people I was going to face, timidly and hopefully, upon getting off the plane. I knew that they— foreigners, Americans—were bound to be different. How would I describe them? Americans were friendly and uncertain. They smiled a lot. They were evasive. They had no right or reason to tell me that nothing in my life was any of my business. They seemed quite willing to leave me alone.

They were confusing.

I began to yearn to go back.

But I knew, of course, that I couldn't go back, because I had already left.

I settled down in Boston. This, I was told, was the most European of all American cities.

Soon I began to feel sleepy all the time and to fall asleep whenever I didn't have to stay awake.

Life was slow.

I slept, and I slept. There was love and pain galore in my dreams. Waking up, I looked around incredulously and saw that I had a place to sleep; I had a room. It was small.

On the other, hot and humid, gasoline fume-filled side of my open window, six tall floors below, sweating, strongly built, hoarse Boston cab drivers yelled at each other. The honking of their horns made me nauseous. Fat women laughed shrilly. Someone was shouting incessantly, "George! George!" People lived happily everywhere; there was a continuity to their lives.

Each of them believed, of course, that only his or her life was important!

It never ceased to strangely surprise me that none of them knew anything about *my* life, as if I didn't have one or wasn't trying hard enough to keep it afloat. But I did have a life. I didn't have to be ashamed of myself.

I looked for a job and then found one in a bookstore, where everything reminded me of how temporary life is. Then I lost it due to my inexplicable sleepiness. I borrowed money from my American roommates; I paid the rent, bought food, ate, pitied myself, slept.

I knew, of course, that I could just as well die up there in my room and no one would notice.

I kept writing letters back home in my mind.

As I lay sleeping, sick of tirelessly listening through the open window to a torrent of words that I couldn't understand, it occurred to me that the people who spoke the same language, even if they despised each other and each other's choice of words, couldn't help at least getting along well with each other. Their hating each other couldn't be anything but a game, played out in all earnestness, of course, yet still destined to end at any moment by a jaunty wink, as in the game of "who-blinks-first."

People who spoke the same language had to be good to each other.

I had slowly come to appreciate the oak-paneled officials' honest, unswerving Russianness in my sleep.

Ashamed of myself, I missed even the most unpleasant of my ex-fellow countrymen!

It occurred to me, further, that two men couldn't honestly misunderstand or be genuinely angry with one other, because they were both men, and neither could two women, unless, of course, those men and women spoke different languages and couldn't share their memories with each other.

"What a bizarre idea!" I thought.

No noise from the street could wake me up. I slept for days on end, becoming good at remembering and memorizing my memories. I realized that I had lived a long life. Good things happened to me in my dreams.

In one dream I was shyly standing in the yellow shadow of an old cast-iron lantern on the quiet Leningrad street in front of the time-worn house where I was born, surrounded by other seven year olds and looking intently at a shiny black grass snake slowly slithering across the wet glistening asphalt a foot away from our feet while its owner, a girl whose name I couldn't recall—and then, of course, I would recall it; it was Nadya—was telling us in a whisper how poisonous her harmless snake was.

In another, I was playing badminton in the red brick back yard of our house on a sunny afternoon filled with sharply edged shadows and strong wind from the Baltic: there were white bedsheets hanging from the thick gray clothesline strung across the back yard that thunderously flapped in the wind. That was at least three years before Yuri Gagarin's space flight. I was wearing someone else's red woolen vest. I leaned against the wet wall of our house and looked at my mother solemnly approaching me with a white cloth sack in her hands. She said, "This is your brother," and shoved the sack in my face.

In yet another dream, my unsteady, stumbling feet kept getting stuck in the damp sand of Lake Razliv's empty beach strewn with rotting weeds and cigarette butts, for which I didn't yet know the word in my language. My grandmother was holding my hands firmly. Someone kept asking me annoyingly how old I was. I couldn't speak, nor would I have wanted to even if I could, so she proudly answered for me: "He's a year and a half." Then a red face with a drooping mustache suddenly lowered itself down to the level of my eyes and, dangerously enlarged, smiled at me. A hoarse voice said: "I used to know Lenin himself when he was hiding out in the village of Razliv just before the Revolution, forty years ago!"

Of course, my memory kept all the dirt and shame out of my dreams.

On a chair by my bedside I kept a piece of paper and a pencil, so that upon waking I could promptly, hastily, write down something, anything—a thought or a dream—which I never did.

I knew that my dreams were too inconclusive for words and my thoughts were too wordy to be worth the effort.

My roommates were shouting at each other in English out in the corridor.

I could barely understand them.

I had come to realize that nothing can be more ruinous to someone's self-esteem than a foreign language that he knows well enough to speak. It goes directly to his head, like champagne bubbles, and he becomes hopelessly overwhelmed by the private power to communicate with native speakers.

They smile at him. They pat his shoulder.

"You speak English very well!" they say.

But he is no fool. He can't help constantly listening to himself. He begins to suspect that other people laugh secretly at his accent; that they find it *cute*. He misses his own language as if it were a dead friend.

He realizes that speaking one's own language is a luxury akin to normal breathing: one takes it for granted until one develops asthma.

Talking to my roommates, asking them for money, I

kept reminding myself that none of my friends back home had ever spoken as much English as I spoke now.

I had the right to feel proud.

I realized that I was a bad listener: I paid too much attention to the words. I tried to keep silent, feeling angry and sorry for those who would never know how many important things I could have told them if only they had bothered to learn Russian.

I discovered that English was making me ill. I knew that like many uncertain people, I had always been quick to judge others' wit, if not their intelligence, by the smoothness of their speech.

I had always oriented myself toward the clarity of hasty assumptions.

But now I just didn't have much to go by!

I didn't like myself, speaking English. I could hear my own heavy accent.

I didn't like my roommates, because their English was so much better than mine.

I realized that every American was a smoother talker than I.

Everyone had the right to think that he was also *smarter* than I! This thought drove me to utter despair. I panicked.

Life was turning out to be too much hard work.

Indeed, before judging someone's wit, I had to translate his words in my own mind quickly, and then search for the words in English. That took all the joy out of the conversation.

Concentrating on the words, I couldn't tell if I liked the man or not, whether the woman had a nice or an ugly voice: all voices sounded foreign to me.

All faces looked the same.

I knew that I was beginning to fall ill. Everything around me seemed sterile. The grass was green, but it looked gray and exuded the odor of gasoline. The trees had no shadows.

People in the streets were awkwardly affecting the pleasure of being happy. I didn't want their lives.

When I was not asleep, I walked the streets of Boston, occasionally glancing down at my wristwatch. I started having headaches.

I felt impatient and tense all the time. What was supposed to amuse me scared me.

Once, standing in a grocery checkout line, I felt unwell and picked up a newspaper from the rack, to find out what was going on back home.

"My home is *here!*" I reminded myself, as always.

"Who am I kidding?" I thought.

The newspaper was called *World Weekly News* and featured the pictures of two men, Gorbachev and someone whose face I didn't know—it was Bill Cosby—quizzically looking at each other across the enormous front-page headline that read: "Bill and Gorbachev—Relatives?"

I glanced around. No one was looking at me. I felt fear.

I realized that finally, quietly, I must have lost my mind. Then I remembered that those who lose their minds usually are the last to notice.

This was a newspaper for American fools!

The days dragged on.

I was sitting in a Harvard Square cafe one afternoon, reading a newspaper from back home, when a young woman whom I had met before, in a bookstore, walked over to my table, smiled at me, and told me that she was celebrating her thirtieth birthday.

"You still look young," I said politely. She nodded.

There was a pause. I felt sleepy with nervousness. I couldn't understand whether I liked her or not.

She spoke English too well.

I didn't like her.

She sat down and ordered wine. We started talking about me.

She said that if she were me, she would never have dared to leave her home for good, knowing that she probably would never see her friends and parents again.

"That's life," I said. What else could I say? I smiled disarmingly; bitterly.

She said that she hated open spaces and rooms with no doors and was always quietly looking around in search of a secluded place, her own private hideout, for fear that they—whoever *they* might be—would suddenly come marching in and round up the Jews. I stared at her.

She knew that I was Jewish.

I didn't like it that she was trying—preposterously—to find common ground between us.

Of course, I was no longer surprised by the superfluous, almost mindless ease with which some Americans that I knew—and, of course, I didn't know many—opened up to an unsuspecting stranger.

Americans tended to tell too much about themselves.

I knew that in that woman's eyes my foreignness greatly outweighed the importance of my intelligence, and that bothered and annoyed me. I wished she would stop telling me things about her life that possibly made it sound interesting.

I wanted no part of her.

She leaned across the table and said: "I know, you may be thinking that I'm old, but I feel *good* about being thirty, because I keep reminding myself that I could've been dead a long time ago, like everyone else who's already dead! People die so easily! But thank goodness, I'm still alive!" Her eyes gleamed.

"What are you *talking* about?" I said.

We had some wine. Her shoe touched my foot under the table.

Then I felt unwell and left.

I began crossing the square. Halfway across, I stopped.

My heart started to race. I couldn't breathe.

My legs softened and folded under my body like two penknives.

I fell to the gasoline-stained cobblestones, blinking in confusion and fear, thinking that everyone was looking at me.

Drivers yelled at me and honked their horns.

I was lying there, dying, far from home. People stood over my body in silence. I knew they wouldn't let me die, although I suspected they might.

Then the police arrived. Then an ambulance. I was taken to the hospital. An indifferent doctor quickly examined my scared heart.

There was nothing wrong with me.

But I still felt awful!

An hour later I returned to my sixth-floor room and fell ill.

I couldn't get up from bed. I stopped leaving my room. I started fearing open spaces and detesting people's voices. Daylight hurt my eyes. There was never enough air in my lungs. I was cold and hot and shivering with unending panic.

This went on for days, weeks, and months.

I had started to write about my illness, but I had trouble developing an unsympathetic and aloof third-person voice. I pitied myself too much. I decided to wait and see what would happen with me.

"I'm in so much trouble!" I thought.

I kept borrowing money from my American roommates. They would buy me some food. I ate.

I had an old TV in my room. The steady stream of incomprehensible words made me nauseous.

I couldn't read: my eyes were constantly blurry. Besides, reading was a waste of time.

No writer had ever lived my life! No one had gone through my pain!

Books in Russian made me feel sad. Books in English reminded me that my English would never be good enough for me to write in it.

I couldn't write in Russian: it made me too homesick and confused. I knew too many Russian words to choose the right ones.

There was no distance between me and my life in Russian.

But I couldn't write in English either!

But even if I could: all my writing would have inevitably been about pain and misery. I was afraid that these wouldn't make for an interesting story. I had nothing to say. I seemed to know all about myself and nothing about anyone else.

Lying in bed and listening to the rhythms of my heartbeat, I tried to imagine the way people talk or think.

What do they feel when you don't pay attention to their words?

How does it feel to know that you are not talented, not bright, not beautiful, not loved?

I would fall back asleep.

My crumpled bedsheets were ugly. The beads of sweat on my body were disgusting.

It had been a long time since I had left.

I remembered that upon leaving the Soviet Union, many people were strangely anxious not to miss from the airplane's silver window the national boundary beneath the white clouds drifting peacefully across the sky.

It was as if they had hoped to find a difference between adjoining, sojourning clouds: one, still timid and constrained; the other, free to drift and float wherever it pleased.

A man I knew told me that he had asked a flight attendant to bring him a bottle of champagne when the plane flew over the neutral zone.

As for me, I had fallen asleep shortly after take-off. When

I awoke, it was already night. I looked out the window.

A radiant net of lights spread over the black land below. It looked like Rio de Janeiro for some reason.

We were about to begin the descent. I turned from the window. No one was looking at me. I put on the headphones, but there was no music.

The plane suddenly roared.

I knew that this was a moment to remember.

I thought about Rio de Janeiro again.

I had read that it was almost as beautiful as Leningrad.

I remembered a documentary about a carnival in Rio that had appeared not long before on Leningrad TV.

The narrator, a tall Englishman whose voice had been replaced by that of an invisible Russian actor, leaned easily against a hilltop balustrade that gave onto the shining bay in the night. The city was full of raucous music and glittering lights. Brightly illuminated yachts stood still on the quiet surface of dark-golden water.

The man smiled into the camera and said in Russian: "I'm young. I'm in Rio. Life is beautiful."

Then he shrugged and smiled, as if to say, "Big deal!"

There was a pause.

"So! I'm still in Rio!" he said.

This time his voice was tinged with impatience.

I knew the feeling. I've had it before.

I lay staring at the ceiling of my sixth-floor room in Boston.

I was falling asleep and then waking.

I was angry with myself. There was not a single story in any of my dreams and memories!

Loud voices came from the street. People were laughing, traveling, having a good time. I, too, wanted to have fun and be happy. I wanted to be among them.

And yet, none of them was going to stay alive forever.

I thought: "You just wait! I'll show you!" I shook my helpless fist at the world.

My roommates shuffled along the corridor. The air smelled of warm dampness.

People lived their lives and died on the flickering TV screen.

Someone was probably still thinking about me back home.

Time went by.

A year later I was riding on a Boston-bound suburban bus on a weekday afternoon. I had of late begun to feel good enough to begin stepping out from my room.

Having gingerly come down the stairs, I would take brisk walks along the quiet streets.

And so I asked one of my roommates to drive me thirty miles from the city and drop me off at one of the suburban bus stops, so that I could learn to make it back to Boston on my own.

The insides of the bus smelled of gasoline. I was nauseated, but my spirits were high. I was proud of myself.

I knew that although I often felt like dying, I had probably already hit bottom and was beginning to slowly move back up, like a volleyball that remains under water only as long as someone's hand keeps it there.

I glanced around. The bus was nearly empty. I smiled.

It occurred to me that none of the people in the bus knew that I was different from them.

I could think in Russian!

This thought, of course, made me feel ashamed for my shallowness. I reminded myself that I couldn't think in *English*.

But then, I rarely thought in words at all.

My English had improved over the past months of

sleeping and TV watching. Now it was probably better than almost any other Soviet emigré's. But the only people who might possibly have noticed or appreciated it were my roommates, and we barely, rarely talked, even though I had started giving Russian lessons at home to a group of college students and had paid my roommates back all the money I had borrowed from them.

No one knew, of course, that there were four voluminous notebooks, several hundred pages filled with stories sitting on the floor in my room. They were written in a mixture of two languages.

When I couldn't find a proper word in the language that I knew worse, I borrowed it from the one that I knew better. The difference between better and worse was vast.

I knew that the stories I had written were bad. None of them had a believable ending, or a credible beginning. All of them dealt with my life.

I was sick and tired of my life.

The bus was nearing Boston.

It had been a long time since I had last seen a city, and it was good to be approaching one. It was like waking in the morning and knowing that Grandfather would take you to the zoo, full of sad and dirty animals, in the afternoon.

There were high-rises and street markets swarming with people in the distance. The viaducts were breathtaking. Business helicopters crossed the sky with great speed.

The pallid-bellied Goodyear blimp was radiant in the sun.

I closed my eyes and pictured palm trees and guavas, and a warm tropical sea full of roaring seashells.

That, of course, was an endearing, slightly-out-of-focus snapshot of a sunlit carnival from a permanently open children's book on a cracked three-legged dinner table in a small room in a large Leningrad communal apartment where someone—it was me!—was playing "Fidel's Barbodas'

March" incessantly, bored, on an old untuned piano and the rancid stench of combi-fat floated in bluish spirals down the corridor, dark, narrow, and littered with shreds of the ancient newsprint that papered the walls.

I looked around. Everyone in the bus was asleep.

And so, too, was I.

I turned back to the window and looked at the wet wall, covered with gray moss, of an empty dark house protruding like a cavernous tooth into the tall blue sky over the tops of the pine trees in late March. It's the time of year when there's still snow on the outskirts of the city, when it's still dark and most people prefer to stay at home in the evening, in their dusky apartments with ceramic stoves decorated with the sentimental motif of Peter the Great, a Dutch pipe in his mouth, striding along.

I have lived in those apartments.

I turned away from the window.

I knew that I couldn't yet handle the excitement of joyous recognitions.

I tried to concentrate on my breathing.

It was pleasant to be daydreaming.

I have always dreamt shyly of a lackadaisical tropical carnival: people wandering around multicolored streets. Someone's room is light and cool in the lazy breeze from the sea beyond the white gauze curtains.

The bus roared.

I awoke and fell back asleep.

As Boston outside the bus window drew nearer and turned real, my excitement subsided. It gave way to sadness and fear.

The city suggested crowded open spaces where I couldn't yet be without instantly feeling ill and hopelessly and helplessly low.

I had a long way to go before safely arriving home, at my sixth-floor room!

The bus was already pulling into the station.

I got off the bus and, just another man in the street, began walking toward the subway. The weather had changed; now the sky was gray and heavy. The air smelled of gasoline and pained my lungs.

At the entrance to the subway station a loud-mouthed teenager in ketchup-splattered overalls was selling shish kebab and shriveled grilled Italian sausage from his smoking mobile cart clouded with soot. I stood watching him for a while.

Then, feeling nauseated, I bought a greasy sausage and began to eat it.

I knew that, of course, I would soon become ill with a stomachache and the disgust and fear of a panic attack.

I kept gobbling up the dripping meat, hot with its melting fat, and so did several other people near me. They seemed to be enjoying themselves.

I knew that I, too, seemed to be enjoying myself. They paid no attention to me.

As I stood there, eating with dignity in the heart of an American city, I wished that someone would suddenly recognize me. But no one in Boston knew me, and I didn't know anyone either.

I glanced at my wristwatch: it was rush hour.

There were so many people in the streets that it was unpleasant to realize that each one of them might have a life of his own.

Of course, I knew that each of them was convinced that his or her life was more important than mine.

I finished the sausage and, instead of hastily heading home on the green "T," took the red-line train to Harvard Square. It had been a long time since I had last taken the subway.

Soon I was at the place where the ambulance car had picked me up after I had collapsed in a fit of fear a year earlier. The square looked the same, probably because I wasn't looking around. I was concentrating hard on my breathing.

I sat down on the bench near Harvard University's cast-iron fence. People were everywhere.

Night came down upon the city, squeezing crowds of tourists onto the streets. I remembered that I had always liked the dark. I got up off the bench and started walking around the square.

I kept my eyes on the entrance to the subway station. My head was aching with dizziness. I would have been surprised if it weren't. When I strayed too far from the subway, a jolt of panic would force me back within the radius of a breathless rush toward its foul-smelling safety.

I knew that once I was on a train heading home, I would start wondering whether maybe I should return to the place from which I had fled.

It was pleasant to realize that I knew so well what to expect from my fear!

And so I walked around the square feeling tense, but also proud of myself. I stopped by small crowded bars and cafes, cautiously stepping inside, ordering nothing, because, of course, I knew that I had to proceed slowly at teaching myself anew, step by step, all the simple gestures of daily living.

I had yet to learn to be surrounded by people.

I couldn't yet drink or eat in public.

I'd just smile back at the polite waiters and waitresses in cafes and bars, shrug, and look around. I'd step inside, registering in my mind each small, almost embarrassingly small triumph, hastily, like a dog hurrying to lift his leg at every tree before he feels a yank on his neck.

An hour had gone by.

I told myself that I'd go home soon.

Confidently making my way through the crowd, I knew

that I looked like every other leisurely man out that night. Yet I also realized that I was merely affecting leisureliness: I was marking time, trying to appear relaxed.

I kept telling myself that nothing bad had happened to me so far.

Other people just seemed to be enjoying themselves.

Soon I noticed that my laps around the square had become smaller. I was getting tired. I stared at my feet.

I heard loud words spoken in Russian with the distinctive aplomb of the oak-paneled officeholders.

I looked up with a start and saw the unmistakable faces. Three Russian men passed me. I turned to follow them. They were walking slowly, talking loudly, almost shouting, as if they were wearing headphones full of deafening music.

They thought no one in the crowd could understand them!

I knew the feeling.

And so I listened to their conversation for a while. They were discussing their meal in a Cambridge restaurant. They seemed to like American food!

I was taken aback. I didn't expect to see them here.

"How odd!" I thought.

With all the changes that had taken place back home since I'd left, one might think that these dubious, unpolished types would have been pushed aside by the new breed of Gorbachevites. One would expect them to have vanished into the black hole of Soviet history. Yet here they were, just where I was.

Weasels.

I remembered sitting once in a beer bar in Leningrad with a friend of mine who was telling me about his recent trip to one of the large provincial cities in central Russia. A group of local officials had been caught unaware by the abrupt change of power. They had lost their jobs and their offices with Lenin's picture on the wall.

One might think that all they had to do was forget about their past and start again, as most other people would have done. But *they*, of course, had done no such thing.

They committed suicide, all of them, because they couldn't forget about the good lives that they had once had!

Whitney Houston's sugary voice, coming from the open window of a record store, soared triumphantly over the square.

I looked at the sturdy backs of the survivors in front of me.

I quickened my pace and caught up with them.

"How's the Party doing, comrades? How are our secret police doing?" I asked in an unnaturally loud voice.

Immediately I felt ashamed of my flippancy.

Suddenly I realized that I no longer felt either love or loathing for them.

That discovery filled me with gleeful joy.

They stopped and stared at me.

"Are you, too, a tourist?" one of them uncertainly asked. I nodded.

"This may well be a provocation," another man said sternly.

"You don't live here, do you?" the third man asked. I shook my head.

Their eyes glazed over as they looked at me with cold condescension.

"Are you out of your mind, young man?" said the first man.

I thought: "Haven't I seen him before?"

It would be interesting, if, unexpectedly, I had recognized him from one of the previous, shameful conversations in which I had begged in his office that he give me permission to leave.

But, of course, I had never seen him before.

I didn't know what to say.

"You're all pathetic idiots!" I said defiantly. They laughed.

Then they walked away.

Dizziness and nausea finally caught up with me. I realized that I had been in the open square for too long.

"Oh my God!" I thought in panic.

I turned around and hurried to the subway station.

I glanced at my wristwatch and saw that I had been out of my room for almost the entire day.

The time had come for me to start wandering aimlessly in more distant neighborhoods. I needed to prove myself a normal survivor.

There were thousands of streets in Boston.

My leisure became a grueling full-time job.

Pretending that I could live a life wasn't easy. Returning back home, I would collapse on the bed and fall asleep. There were days when I couldn't get out of bed. There were days when I couldn't wake up.

After a few months of fearful hesitation I decided that I should try staying overnight at some friendly place, with someone who would be aware of my circumstances.

It had to be someone who wouldn't be surprised if I woke him up in the middle of the night, panicked and begging him to call the ambulance.

I called a Russian friend of a good Russian friend of mine from home. He had left a year before me. Needless to say, his life had been hard ever since.

We had many things in common. He rented a room in a five-room apartment, not far from where I lived. We had been talking over the phone ever since I came to Boston, yet I had never met him. He was my age.

I came to his place late one night. He opened the door, looking sleepy. We went to the kitchen and sat there, talking, for several hours, drinking decaffeinated tea.

We didn't have any friends from home in Boston. We liked each other.

His roommates—they were Spanish—were sound asleep when he took me to the living room and told me that I could spend the night on the couch.

I looked around. The room was nearly empty. There was a large fish tank in the corner, dark with murky water slowly whirling around dirty pink, multi-turreted, Gothic castles made of seashell shards.

"Fish!" I said.

He shrugged his shoulders apologetically and said, "My roommates. They're Spanish. They can't live without a little *corrida.*"

I walked over to the tank where a flock of small transparent tropical fishes darted about behind the thick glass.

Two larger fish, flat and almost round, owlish, pewter gray, with blood-tinged gills and bulldog jaws studded with rows of sharp colorless triangular teeth, hovered calmly in the dark glutinous water, half hidden in a corner behind one of the castles, like robbers in an ambush.

"Piranhas," the new friend of mine said, reverently lowering his voice and looking at them with disgust. "They bought them for a hundred dollars apiece, because they're against-the-Massachusetts-law fish. Owning them is like betting on dog fights. But they never attack their prey when the lights are on, and they always know when someone's watching them!"

I pressed my forehead against the glass and saw that the bottom of the tank was littered with open-mouthed heads of small fish.

"Imagine what's going on in those little ones' heads," he said, smiling. "I mean those who are still alive. They've seen their friends go. They know what's going to happen to them. They know what they're in there for. They're no dummies. But they've got nowhere to hide. Look at those castles—they've got no *doors!*"

"That's pretty clever," I said.

I got undressed, turned off the light, and laid down on the couch. The street behind the window was quiet. The place was dark. Only occasional cars outside, speeding by with excessive roaring, illuminated the ceiling.

I felt tense.

Listening to the silence of the carnage that was taking place in the fish tank, I knew that I wouldn't be able to fall asleep.

Then I opened my eyes and sleepily lifted my arm. The flourescent dial of my wristwatch floated brightly in the weightless dark. Three hours had gone by while I was asleep. It was the darkest hour of the night.

Someone was in the room, standing in the corner at the fish tank.

I raised my head from the warm pillow and saw a tall young man stooped down in the corner. His forehead was pressed against the glass of the tank.

I watched him for a while.

He turned his head to me and gave me a friendly smile that looked, because it was dark in the room, like a warning. His eyes were glistening.

Then he tiptoed out of the room and I fell back asleep.

I decided the next morning to stay in that room for several more nights. It was so repulsive that, of course, I knew: nothing could have put my ill stamina to a better test.

Every morning there were several more severed fish heads on the silty bottom of the tank.

"How can you put up with this?" I asked my friend.

He just shrugged helplessly: "You've got to be flexible

and tolerant. You've got to have respect for other people's quirks. We're not in Russia anymore."

Then I returned home, fell down on the bed, and slept for two days.

I started spending most of my time at my friend's place. We talked and reminisced.

I seriously nodded when he would say, bitterly, that the world wasn't giving us the credit we deserved.

One day, when he had stepped out to the grocery store, I saw a stack of leaflets and homemade books expounding on the inherent vileness of the Jews sitting on his desk.

Of course, I was so upset at first that it didn't even occur to me that he might have left them lying around on purpose, for me to see.

Then I realized that it just couldn't be: we were *friends*.

I thought: "I've been spending time with the wrong person!"

I almost cried with disappointment. What a waste of time!

This had already happened to me once before, when I was in the eighth grade.

I had an older friend back then. I helped him with his homework and he taught me how to drink without getting drunk. We spent most of our time together.

He even showed me the stories that he wrote: they were bad. I never showed him mine.

Then we both fell in love with the same girl and, sitting one night in our schoolyard, felt so much alike and in tune with each other that our tormented souls seemed to be hovering in the warm air overhead, intertwined, like two tender, bluish rings of smoke blending into the color of the late-spring Leningrad sky.

"You're my friend," he said solemnly, "and that prevents me from telling you that it'd be far more fair if I got the girl, if she'd take me, because the Jews already have the entire world in their pocket!"

At first I was so upset that it didn't even occur to me that he'd meant it to be a compliment.

That was a long time ago.

As I recall, he even looked a little like my ex-friend from Boston!

I've always believed that people who say, or do, or think the same things can't help at least resembling each other.

And so, of course, I had to stop visiting the apartment with the fish tank.

It was sad at first, to feel disappointed in someone. Then it occurred to me that every time I lost a friend because he had suddenly revealed himself to be a fool, my sadness had a distinctive aftertaste of pleasure.

It was pleasant to know that there was something in my character that wouldn't let me be friends with someone who didn't deserve it.

"Forget about him!" I told myself.

But the ex-Soviet man, unaware that I had seen the books and the leaflets in his room, kept calling me. He needed a friend.

I had nothing to say to him and each time couldn't wait to finish the conversation.

Returning to my solitude wasn't easy. Life became slow again.

After a week or two of steadily growing independence, when I would begin thinking that I probably could go anywhere, like anyone else, a strong backlash of pain and sadness would inevitably, each time unexpectedly, knock me back down on my bed.

I would lie there, gasping for air and sweating, scared and wishing that I could cry with humiliation. I would try to convince myself that in a week I would forget all about my present weakness.

One day, when I was feeling low and could barely walk, my former friend called me to say that the fish in the tank in his living room were dead because no one had bothered to clean the tank. The weeds had taken over the water and absorbed all the oxygen.

He sounded upset.

I imagined two dead piranhas, bloated and ugly, like wrecked battleships, their snouts stuck in the rich silt fertilized with blood and blood-stained fish scales on the bottom of the tank.

"I'm sorry to hear that," I said, feeling a little better because of the effort I had to make to keep listening.

He probably decided that we still were friends.

"That's no big deal!" he said. "Look, I've just bought an old car. Let's drive to New York!"

Nausea was giving me a headache. I thought about him, his car, and New York.

"I don't know. I'm afraid," I said. "I'm afraid I can't. Oh, what the hell, let's go!"

He said he would pick me up in a week.

Immediately I felt disgusted with myself because, of course, I couldn't *stand* the guy anymore!

When I thought that I would have to sit in his car for five hours, I felt like throwing up.

Then I felt scared: I knew that going to New York might mean pushing the slow luck of my tentative recovery too far. I knew that, with or without dignity, I would have to survive the *road* to New York.

Then I would have to endure at least *one day* in New York!

New York was full of open spaces. It was the ultimate challenge. Having faced and met it, I would, at least, have nothing more to worry about. I hoped so. I knew the capricious nature of my illness.

I couldn't decide whether I had to confront my ex-friend

and tell him that I didn't like people who hated Jews.

I thought—I knew—that I wouldn't sleep for several nights before the trip to New York. However, instead of insomnia, I had one nightmare after another.

They were the kind of dreams that are not supposed to be remembered.

On the other hand, I couldn't forget them either.

Unable to wake, I tried to laugh them off in my sleep. It didn't work. They were too disturbing.

In these dreams, I was inflicting pain on someone whom I had hurt before. Waking up, I couldn't help being angry with myself. I kept telling myself, soothingly, that at least the guy who would be driving me to New York knew about my unpredictable fear. And I would have to expect kind and comforting words from someone I couldn't stand anymore.

I thought: "Why am I doing this to myself? Why can't I just take a train to New York?"

There had to be a serious flaw in my character.

I had friends from back home in New York.

One of them, a young actress, had left Leningrad just a year ago and now lived in Manhattan with her American girlfriend from the South.

They were both looking for acting jobs, supporting themselves in the meantime by waiting tables in a profitable ethnic restaurant. They rented a railroad flat.

When I told her on the phone that I was coming to New York, she invited me to stay with them for a while.

"There's plenty of room!" she kept saying. "Lots of room and just one real bed!"

"Sounds good!" I said.

I didn't know what a railroad flat was supposed to look like, but I loved the way it sounded. I have spent half of my

life on trains, traveling through the vast open spaces of
Russia. In college I even worked as a conductor, staying
awake twenty hours a day for weeks, many years ago. I had
missed trains and railroads ever since I had left Leningrad.

We left Boston early in the morning, my ex-friend and I.
We hardly exchanged a dozen words in five hours.

Like anything fearfully anticipated, the drive went well,
and I knew that I had handled it with dignity. When I
climbed out of the car in New York, on Broadway, I felt
calm and in control. He and I didn't shake hands or promise to stay in touch. He drove away.

I knew, of course, that soon I would become ill with
anxiety and hurried to the nearest phone booth.

The girl from Leningrad was not in her railroad flat,
although she was supposed to have been waiting for my
call.

People were everywhere. Their faces were blank. I began
walking in a New York crowd.

I had seen that faceless crowd many times gloomily
advancing on the camera on the black-and-white TV news
in my room in Leningrad.

Now I was in New York myself! I took a deep breath.

"So far so good!" I thought.

It was reassuring to know that if I were to collapse right
there on Broadway, my body would immediately stop the
flow of disinterested passersby.

I walked for a while. Soon I felt nauseated and scared.
I couldn't see.

I stopped, stepped to the side, and sat on the sidewalk,
strewn with butts and shreds of newsprint, next to a tall
black man in a knit cap with his eyes closed.

I leaned my back against the sooty wall of some old
frame house.

I felt like just another homeless man on TV.

It occurred to me, of course, that a TV camera from home might eventually take a picture of my side of the sidewalk.

I thought: "Maybe my friends back in Leningrad will see me with my back against the wall the very next night on TV!"

I tried to picture their disbelief and excitement when they saw me.

In the meantime, my racing heart couldn't be calmed. I was too far away from my room.

I pulled my address book out of my pocket and scribbled my name and my parents' Leningrad home phone number in ugly capital letters on the first page.

I tried to calm myself.

I told myself that I had already died many times in my fear. One more death would be nothing new.

"Who am I kidding?" I thought.

People nonchalantly stepped over my stretched out legs as I concentrated on my breathing with my eyes closed.

Then I felt someone's hand on my shoulder and opened my eyes.

The man who was sitting on the sidewalk next to me looked at me with sympathy: "You all right, man?"

I felt like leaning my head on his shoulder.

"Talk to me, man!" he said.

He looked away and started talking to another man who was standing in front of him. They were jiving. I couldn't understand a word.

"Spare a dollar, man," the man said, turning back to me.

"I don't understand," I said, shrugging.

He frowned: "You don't, huh? But you will, won't you, my good man?"

He put his hand on my shoulder again. I quickly got
up off the asphalt.

Angry and scared, I walked for a long time. Then I
turned left at an intersection, heading west.

I have never been good at orienting myself in unfamiliar places but, of course, I knew that I couldn't get any more
lost in New York than I already was. I kept walking.

My unswerving trancelike stride made several hurrying passerbys bump into me.

One old man, looking mad, purposely hit me with his
shoulder. Then he stopped, smiled, and gave me the finger.

"Old man, you shouldn't be so angry, you don't have
much time left to live!" I said, smiling.

Instantly I felt ashamed.

I kept trying to reach the girl in the railroad flat on the
phone, but no one was there. Still, I knew that sooner or
later I'd find my way to her safe place.

I wasn't alone in this city.

Besides, the worst was probably already behind me. I
kept walking.

When I felt too unwell to see where I was going, I would
stop, thinking in despair, "Oh my God! I'm in so much
trouble!" That odd mantra never failed to comfort me.

It was reassuring to realize that if I could still think in
words, and in foreign words at that, then, of course, I was
in complete control of myself.

Soon I began feeling better. I started paying attention
to the numbers on the streets and avenues.

They were less unfamiliar to me than I had expected.

When I found myself in the West 20s, I remembered
that an American girl that I had known well years ago, in
Leningrad, lived someplace nearby.

Once, when we were making love in my Leningrad
apartment, I whispered something passionate in English in

her ear and immediately felt her become tense. She pushed me away.

"What's wrong?" I asked, puzzled. She said accusingly: "If you can speak English now, that means you're just *faking* making love! That means you're *thinking!*"

But I just wanted to be good to her; I just wanted to make her feel good!

I found her phone number in my address book and dialed it. She wasn't home either.

Finally I managed to reach the girl that invited me to stay with her. She sounded glad to hear my voice.

I took the dank subway to her place.

Leaning up against the door in the rocking, roaring car, I sensed the familiar menace in the glances of the passengers.

In twenty minutes I was in front of her house. It was already dark. The door was blocked by a group of sinister-looking men and women.

As I drew nearer, they stopped talking. One of them, unsteady on his feet, stepped forward and winked at me.

I smiled back. He frowned.

I glanced down at my wristwatch.

"Looking for a smoke, sir?" asked a young woman in a giddy voice. She wasn't ugly.

She had an ugly wart on her face.

I shook my head. The people around her were staring at me.

I looked at the darkly lit doorway: my friend was supposed to have come downstairs and opened the door for me five minutes ago.

"Would you be interested in a blow job for under two bucks, sir?" the woman asked. I stared at her.

She smiled and winked at me.

I turned away. She laughed.

I knew that if I opened my mouth, these people probably wouldn't like my accent.

"Two bucks is a reasonable price," the woman said.

I shrugged.

"What are you, depressed or something?" she asked.

I looked at her with hope and nodded.

"Then maybe a little suck would help, sir," she said.

"That's right! You should listen to her!" said one of the men.

"Not from you, lady!" I said. She laughed again.

I felt ashamed.

"Where you from, man?" one of the men asked.

I stepped toward the door. The people in front of me silently moved aside.

I saw my girlfriend coming down the stairs. She opened the door, smiling. I walked inside.

We hugged and kissed.

The people on the other side of the door booed.

"She's *worse* than me!" laughed the woman with a wart. "Worse and a whole lot more *expensive!*"

"What's all that about?" the girl asked.

Her railroad flat was on the second floor. Two rooms were separated by the absence of a door.

The apartment did, indeed, look like a train car. It was cluttered, littered, and dark.

There was a bed in one room and a couch in another, where the TV was.

My friend's roommate, a young and pretty American girl, had a Southern accent that was heavy enough for me to discern instantly.

Two fat, neutered cats, Ed and Brad, walked lazily around the kitchen, their stiff tails shuddering in nervous anticipation of food.

We had a glass of wine. It had been two years since I

had last tasted wine. Then the girls suggested that we go out for a walk around midtown Manhattan.

I realized that they didn't have many friends in this city. They were so happy, so glad to see me!

And who was I?

It was already night outside, and I felt good. I couldn't imagine having ever been fearful.

As we walked out, the people still leaning up against the wall began laughing and catcalling.

One of them shouted something that made the rest of them cheer wildly.

The American girl shook her head and furtively glanced at me. Of course, neither I nor the girl from Leningrad understood what the man had said.

Looking back, I saw that two men were following us.

We quickened our pace and crossed the street. In five minutes we were on Broadway.

We stopped by some small bar, sat down at the corner table, and had some more wine while pensively looking at the red brick walls.

People's faces were animated in the trembling candle-light. Quick shadows moved behind the weightless threads of bamboo over the open door to the adjacent room.

There was cigarette smoke in the air. Someone chuckled ironically in back of me.

I felt quiet joy.

It was pleasant to know that the time would come when I, too, would be able to sit every night in some, always the same, New York bar, talking with my friends and friendly strangers and listening to the sad saxophone of a cool sad man in a shiny suit in the corner in the wee hours of the morning. Then I'd walk back to my place, which would be small and crowded with books, glancing kindly, conde-scendingly at the sleeping windows, all dark, unlike the night windows in Leningrad, which are forever glowing with the blue circles of little flames above the gas stove in a kitchen where a fat bare-chested man hugs his disheveled wife in a pink nightgown as they both stare at your window right across the street.

I would climb the narrow stairs and unlock my door. Then I would sit down at my desk and, slightly drunk and pleasantly tired, begin writing, thinking, of course, of how fortunate I was to have worked things out in my life so that I could live it merely by remembering and describing it, endlessly, until the very end of my days.

The girls pulled at my sleeve.

We left the bar.

Soon we came to Times Square, the throbbing nerve of sleaze and excess on the black-and-white news on an old TV in a crummy room in the dark on the outskirts of Leningrad.

I looked around.

It occurred to me that here, in the heart of the greatest, most powerful city in the world was the best and the worst of what this world had to offer me.

I was old enough to stop looking for a better city to live. I already knew that life was too short to have lived everywhere. Why, then, take less than the center of the world?

"Who would've thought?" I thought, a little ashamed of my excitement.

I realized that we had walked far away from the railroad flat. I began to feel overwhelmed by all the shouting, shoving, and screaming. We walked some more and I relaxed.

We dropped by another bar and had some more wine.

On the way back home the American girl stopped to make a call to a man with whom she used to go to junior high. He had just moved to New York and rented an apartment nearby.

"I want to show you how *some* people live in this city," she said.

Her friend was home and invited us over. He lived in a high-rise apartment building with a uniformed doorman and epauletted security servants behind a desk with TV monitors in the lobby.

The elevator was the size of my sixth-floor room in Boston.

His apartment was on the twenty-fifth floor and cost him $3000 a month. He was in his early twenties and had a stupidly disarming smile.

"Welcome to my shabby shack!" he said, beaming.

I realized that he was just a clean-cut boy, not too bright, understandably proud of his luck.

It occurred to me that I'd had a better life behind me than he could ever hope to live: I had seen many more interesting things than he could ever learn from watching movies!

It was unpleasant to realize that I had to feel my superiority over this kid in order to feel good and comfortable in his comfortable, spacious apartment.

He told me that his father was a chairman of an oil corporation in the South and asked me what I thought about Gorbachev.

We had some good wine, although I have never been good at telling good wine from bad wine.

Back home, I used to drink sheer poison.

"Gorbachev!" I said.

I told him that Gorbachev was nice, smooth. He was beautiful, enlightened, bright as a lighthouse!

Immediately I felt ashamed of my flippancy.

The young man was just interested in international affairs!

Soon he got drunk and wanted to know why I wasn't saying anything about his apartment. Did I like it?

I patted him on the shoulder and told him that I was beginning to think, for the first time in my life, that Karl Marx might have been on to something when he suggested slightly redistributing the wealth of a few between many people, until nothing was left of it. He laughed happily.

The girls laughed.

I knew, of course, that my friend from back home, who had become even prettier than she used to be back home, didn't know English well enough to understand my lame joke.

I got up off the sofa and walked over to the window. We were high in the sky over Manhattan. The furious skyline of the center of the world was spread over the illuminated darkness below and above.

The window was open a foot or so, just enough for a tempted man to jump.

I turned away and told the girls that I was tired.

I wasn't tired, but I felt some feverish, unhealthy excitement. The day was catching up with me.

I knew that I would have to pay for it later.

Of course, I was prepared to pay, simply because I knew that I would have no other choice.

And so we left.

When we were in the elevator, I realized that I had already forgotten our host's name.

Then I remembered it: Dan.

"Was that clown's name Dan?" I asked the girls. They nodded.

I knew that I would never meet him again and could forget his name for good.

My memory could use some empty space.

As we walked outside, someone shouted, "Hey, you!" from up above.

We looked up and saw Dan. His head, the size of a thimble, was sticking out of the twenty-fifth floor window.

"Wait up!" he called out. "We'll take a cab! I'm coming too!"

"We only have one bed!" the American girl yelled back.

"That's just what I mean!" he shouted. He was very drunk.

The girls laughed.

For an instant I was afraid that he might fall out of the window. Then his head disappeared into the dark altitude.

"That Dan!" the American girl said, admiringly shaking her head.

I remembered that I'd had nothing to eat since I had left Boston.

I wasn't hungry, but I knew that if I went without food for a day, I would soon have to pay for it.

Food would cost me less.

The street was almost empty when we reached the girls' house. The people who had earlier blocked my way in—and our way out—must have moved to some other place.

Before we went up, I told the girls that I had to find something to eat.

After all, I was a guest and couldn't eat their food.

Besides, there was no food in their house. They had no money and ate at the restaurant where they worked.

I looked around. There were several cafeterias and delis on the block.

One had a modest handwritten sign on the door, "Eat Our Falafel!" The word "falafel" sounded vaguely European, like "Hammeln" or "Fanfan the Tulip." It evoked pleasant childhood memories.

I walked inside. The place was the size of the elevator in the house that we had just left. There was a small man with a drooping mustache behind the counter. I ordered a falafel to go. He shook his head and told me that they were out of falafel. Their hommus was good, though, he added. Hommus sounded less nice than falafel, but it was still better than nothing. I nodded. In a heavy, high-pitched accent, the man shouted something throaty in the direction of the kitchen behind him. Then he turned to me and smiled. I looked around, waiting, thinking of how the three of us would work out the sleeping arrangements on the bed and the couch in the railroad flat. There were three exciting options and one boring one.

I noticed Yasir Arafat's picture on the outer side of the kitchen wall.

"You not American, that's right?" the man asked. I shook my head.

"You European?" he asked. I nodded.

"You Jewish," he said with what sounded like a mild reproach. He smiled.

"That's none of your business!" I said.

He threw his hands up and waved them protestingly. "No-no-no!" he said. "That's all right! Look at me: I'm Jewish myself!"

I looked at him and saw that he wasn't Jewish.

Two more men silently stepped out of the kitchen. They folded their arms on their T-shirted chests and shyly smiled at me.

"Have you ever was in Israel?" asked one of them.

"That's none of your business!" I said again. I was beginning to feel angry.

Another, taller man shook his head: "Why being rude? We simply want to know your opinion if Israel should keep to go on to exist."

I turned and left, angry with myself.

The man who was standing behind the counter rushed after me and grabbed my sleeve: "How about your hommus? You don't want it? We *made* it!"

"Leave me alone," I said.

I felt more awkward than scared.

"Please!" I added.

We stared at each other for a while.

The girls were cheerfully chatting with some people who were standing in front of their door a few feet away.

I waved at them. They waved back.

"Why do you need two girls? You don't need two girls!" said the man. I walked away.

Before falling asleep on the couch in the second room of my friend's railroad flat, I listened to the mighty roar of New York. It reminded me of Moscow.

Leningrad was quieter, of course; more like Boston.

The cats were chasing each other in the kitchen. The girls were giggling in their bed in the dark.

I thought for a while that maybe I should just sneak under their blanket and tell them that I was afraid of the dark.

They probably wouldn't mind.

I looked at my fluorescent wristwatch: it was almost one in the morning.

Soon everything became comfortably silent and warm.

I woke up with a start, instantly and unexpectedly scared. Hastily I pressed my hand against my heart: it was beating steadily.

It was half past three.

I was lying on my back, staring at the ceiling and trying to calm down.

When my eyes became accustomed to the dark, I heard quiet, muffled whispering coming from the girls' bed. They, too, were awake.

They were stirring clinking ice cubes in glasses of water. One of them suddenly laughed.

"Sh-h!" the American girl whispered loudly. "He's asleep. Be quiet!" Maybe they were lovers.

For some reason that thought was unpleasant.

"Maybe he's *not* asleep," the Russian girl said, giggling.

"He's kind of cute," the American girl said loudly.

"He is, isn't he?" said the Russian girl. "But he's *asleep*."

They both laughed.

I realized that, of course, they were just friends.

It was nighttime that was responsible, as always, for making any foolish thought seem plausible.

Soon they fell back asleep. I got up off the bed, cautiously walked to the TV in the corner, and turned it on. It immediately roared and I quickly turned down the sound. For a while a hidden camera recorded two men discussing liquid antacids. Then CBS *Nightwatch* came on and someone gray-haired said, pensively looking into the camera, that in five hundred years Elvis would be more popular than all other public figures of our time put together.

I turned the TV off and returned to bed, thinking that there was no point in ever becoming famous in a world so responsive to dead Elvises.

Besides, even if I were to become an American writer, no one in this country would know my name anyway.

But people back home would. "Can you believe this?" they would say. "Yevgeny Litovtsev has become an American writer! He's writing in *English!*"

I felt pleasantly ashamed of my shallowness.

The cats came galloping in from the kitchen, chasing each other.

One of them, either Ed or Brad, leapt up in the air and landed on my chest like a flour sack.

"Are you out of your mind?" I whispered furiously. He— or it—paid no attention to the anger in my voice. Purring, he began licking his paw. He was heavy.

I considered simply rolling over on my side for an instant, or just pushing him off me, but I have always been meek and humble when someone is acting unceremoniously and with enough self-assurance to make me realize my own weakness, even when that someone is just a cat.

Besides, it was pleasant to realize that the cat had faith in my kindness. I felt as if I had been trying to win his trust for a long time.

The cat was warm, the night was dark. Life was good.

Then I got bored and shook the cat off onto the floor.

It had been a long time since I had been so sleepless at night. Outside the open window cars went by in a steady flow. The November night was warm.

It was probably snowing heavily and silently all over Russia. It was early noon in Leningrad. I lay in the dark, trying to think of what to remember. My mind turned to a man from Leningrad who could have been as famous as Elvis. I remembered having recently read articles about him in a Leningrad newspaper and in a Moscow magazine. In Moscow they were making a documentary about his life. I knew him well. He was a poet, a balladeer; the best among those good-for-nothings, unrepentant in their misery, that flourish freely in the night kitchens of tiny apartments in big cities, drinking and singing through their lives, and then suddenly going up in tender blue flames, like pure alcohol burning in clean glass with a piece of black bread sitting next to it on the table.

They rarely die, however, those young men.

But *he* was dead.

One night we were sitting in the crummy kitchen of the poet's girlfriend's tenth-floor apartment on the outskirts of Leningrad. We were drinking cheap wine and talking. There were five or six of us in the kitchen. It was summer and the night had a lilac color. Even the dull concrete of

boxlike new apartment buildings smelled with the honey-
suckle of burgeoning nostalgia. He sang his fierce, dis-
jointed songs for a while.

He looked and sounded so supernaturally inspired that,
had I not known otherwise, I might have thought that he
was affecting the intense insanity of a singing Russian holy
fool. But, of course, I knew that it was real, and I was jealous. Then he stopped singing. We couldn't think of anything more to do. There was very little wine left in any of
the dark sticky bottles on the table, so we started playing
a fortunetelling game, the half-empty-glass-and-golden-ring
version.

We took a glass, half filled with tap water, and then
the poet's girlfriend slipped a golden ring off her finger and
tied it to a white thread. He wrapped the end of the thread
around his forefinger and lowered the ring down into the
glass, so that it was almost touching the water.

Ironically chuckling, we started asking questions. Each
question had to start with the words "how long": How long
is it going to take me to get a new room? How long is it
going to take Chernenko to die already? How long is it going
to take me to win the lottery?

When someone asked a question, the ringholder nodded solemnly, a mere channeler of the ring's omniscience.
The ring would suddenly begin to sway above the water of
its own accord, slowly at first, and then with gradually
increasing amplitude, until it would hit the side of the glass,
ricochet off it and hit the other side; then again, and again,
each strike meaning a year or a month.

"How long is it going to take us to get married?" the
poet's girlfriend asked, and added, "Don't move your hand!
Don't encourage the ring!"

The ring hit the sides five times.

"Five months," she said contentedly. "Well, that's reasonable."

"How long is it going to take me to become rich?" another girl asked.

"Twenty," said the ring.

"Twenty what?" she asked. Everyone laughed. She pouted.

"Now a *serious* question. How long is it going to take those morons to give me permission to leave?" I said.

"Let's not bore the ring," said the girl who wanted to be rich. I looked at her and saw that she was pretty.

She was one of those girls who had always instantly disliked me for some reason.

The ring started swaying with the force of sheer gleefulness. When it had struck thirty and continued to tirelessly sway, I gave up counting and waved my hand in frustration.

"This is a stupid game," said the poet's girlfriend.

The poet laughed and put his hand on my shoulder. "This is just a piece of gold, man! What does it know about the way a Party hack's mind operates?"

I left Leningrad in less than a year.

Then, a year later, I learned that the poet—then again, he wasn't really a poet!—had committed suicide. He had thrown himself out of the same kitchen window that had been so uninvitingly open on the night of our fortunetelling.

According to a friend's letter, the poet—then again, he wasn't really a poet, but he wasn't really a balladeer either!—had been drinking for several weeks, time after time reaching the point where drunkenness transforms itself into a boring form of sobriety. Then he just walked to the partly open window and, before anyone could see him and grab his sleeve, folded like a penknife and, awkwardly, pushed himself out through the opening.

I had a hard time reading my friend's letter from back home in hot and humid Boston.

Sweating with sticky sickness, I imagined the drunk poet's flight to the dusty, littered bottom of the courtyard. I shuddered.

It occurred to me, as I tried to feel sorrow for someone who was not myself, that he probably didn't even intend to kill himself.

Maybe it was just a spur-of-the-moment, "why not?" wild kind of thing that spontaneous people like him often do.

I could easily see that: you're sitting in the kitchen amid the smells of stale food, in the dark glow of a White Night, surrounded by dirty utensils and half-empty glasses and empty wine bottles. You look around morosely—and the window is ajar.

Slowly you get up off your stool—there were no chairs in that kitchen when I was there—and walk to the window.

Then, of course, this "why not?" thing can't help crossing your mind. It occurs to you that this is something that you have never done before: life has already happened to you, but not death. Because of the uncertain light and the nauseatingly sweet wine in your blood, everything is slow, like in a dream sequence where the action takes place above the clouds on a gray day.

So you just do it. A second before you're on the windowsill, a second after you're nowhere, leaving it to someone else to wonder about the fragility of his own life. The instant is like a membrane: you prick it with a pin and the balloon explodes, the phone stops working, you become deaf, and you know that your heart, too, may explode unpredictably, and that your body can burst with a cancer that it has been nurturing for months, and your plane can come apart high in the sky.

Life is full of menace.

Someone can climb into your open window while you're

listening to someone shrieking out on the street: "George! George!"

It was a woman's voice, filled with fear and anger: "Don't! Don't!" She sounded desperate.

As I listened to her anguished, yet strangely comforting howls, I thought that this probably could be a beginning, or an end, of a story where someone—me—is lying in his bed, reminiscing and worrying about things past and present, while someone else is being killed, or raped, or robbed, or raped *and* robbed, and killed, outside his window, in the quiet background of his sleeplessness.

The woman doesn't really get killed. Nothing bad is going to happen to her. She loves the man. They've been lovers for many years. They're having an argument about his alleged infidelity.

The street suddenly becomes silent. The woman, gently sobbing, timidly smiling, tells the man—whose name is George—"Hold me, George! I love you!"

I wished there had been a pencil and a piece of paper on a chair by my bedside.

It was pleasant to imagine the empty street. I have always loved to listen to the gradual awakening of a city, whenever I was not asleep at night, thinking sleeplessly that while everyone was asleep, I was already awake. I looked at my wristwatch: it was seven in the morning. Four hours had gone by.

With the suddenness of a reminder that I was not in Leningrad anymore—back there, the change of light was always slow—it became light outside.

I got up off the bed and turned on the TV. Lying in bed, I watched *CBS This Morning* with Kathleen Sullivan and Harry Smith for a while, and it felt like Sunday.

Then the crowds of weekday rush-hourers outside filled

the room with a steady din. The sound of blowing horns drifted through the street. I got dressed, quietly, trying not to wake the girls, and tiptoed past them and out the door, leaving it open a crack because I didn't have keys.

It was sunny outside. I made my way through the crowd and ran bouncing across the street, past the policemen and the ambulance surrounded by a dense mob of people in business clothing who were staring down at something sprawled in front of them on the asphalt, blocking the way to cars and buses.

I walked into a German deli across the street and ordered a roast beef sandwich with a salad, and relish, and sauerkraut, and pickles to go.

On the way back I bought *The New York Times, Esquire* magazine with Sam Shepard's picture on the cover, and two cans of Nine Lives cat food.

Back up in the girls' apartment, I unwrapped the sandwich and put some mustard on the dark red meat. Then I opened the refrigerator and found a carton of Tropicana orange juice. I poured it into a glass.

The salad was covered with shuddering beads of water; it smelled like an early breakfast in the Georgian town of Batumi on the Black Sea many years earlier. The pickles were not too sweet.

I read the newspaper and left the magazine, cover up, on the table, so that the girls could have a look at a handsome and sensitive man when they awoke. Then I fed the cats.

The girls were still asleep, their faces fresh and childishly fat without makeup.

It would be a shame, of course, to stay inside on a day like this.

I took a piece of paper and wrote on it, "Be back in an hour. Don't go anywhere. I don't have keys!" in two languages, so that both of them could read it.

Of course, *both* of them could read English.

I ran downstairs, thinking of what to do and where to go.

A heavy dirty bus, waddling like a duck and filled with people, pulled up to the curb and unfolded its doors.

I felt a twinge of fear and uneasiness. For an instant I thought I might be pushing my luck too far. Yet I knew that, of course, I couldn't get lost in Manhattan. I decided that I would get off the bus on the second stop and walk my way back.

I climbed inside.

The bus closed its doors with a hiss.

Squeezed by commuters' shoulders, I gripped the handrail and looked out the window.

We were passing a building made of a shiny mirror; it was on golden fire under the sun.

I quickly combed my hair and looked at myself in the mirror, prepared to be surprised, as always, by the serious maturity of my face.

What I saw instead was just a bus slowly moving along the cluttered sunlit street.

In the mirror I kept searching for my face, but it was lost among the featureless blur of other faces.

I looked around, smiling, wondering if someone else had been struck by this oddity: you look at yourself in the mirror, and all you can see is a faceless busful of faces, and yours is hopelessly lost among them.

A strange feeling.